W9-CME-782

KATHY

by

Edna Moore Schultz

MOODY PRESS
CHICAGO

Original Title:
THEY SAID KATHY WAS RETARDED

Copyright ©, 1963, by
THE MOODY BIBLE INSTITUTE
OF CHICAGO

Moody Paperback Edition, 1972
Reprinted, 1973

ISBN: 0-8024-4525-X

Dedication

There is only one person to whom this book can rightfully be dedicated, the one who shared Kathy's life with me from its beginning until the Palm Sunday evening when she went to her heavenly home. We enjoyed her together, battled for her very life together, prayed for her together and now remember her together. With the deepest gratitude for his patience, his understanding, his utter devotion to Kathy and his constant solicitude, I lovingly dedicate this book to my husband and Kathleen's father, Lieutenant Charles S. Schultz, Police Department, City of Buffalo, New York.

— EDNA MOORE SCHULTZ

Contents

Preface

ONE OF THE GREAT BLESSINGS afforded me by God in my calling and labors as a pastor has been that of knowing Kathy Schultz, one of God's little ones who believed in Him. Hers was a life lived under a handicap permitted by God and designed to glorify Him. Kathy lived her life and fulfilled that purpose before God called her to be with Him to enjoy the beauties of Heaven.

Kathy encouraged my heart many times with four little words that were peculiar to her and described perfectly the life she lived. The four words, accompanied with a curtsy, whether in the home where she was dearly loved or in the church she dearly loved, were: "Pastor—I love the Lord."

Kathy was allowed only a short span of almost nine years, but she lived a lifetime in those years, and her faith in God was a constant source of blessing and encouragement to all who knew the hardship to which the little life was subjected.

To you who read this story, may there be kindled in your hearts a new love and greater faith in Him who doeth all things well.

DONALD A. SWARTZ, Pastor
Prospect Avenue Baptist Church
Buffalo, New York

CHAPTER 1

Kathy is Born—a Mongoloid

THE ZERO HOUR was approaching. The countdown was almost completed. Every woman who has borne a child will remember with a little shudder the time when there was no tomorrow. This was it!

I had been dragging along wearily since the previous Sunday evening, wavering between a sense of urgency and of well-being. By five o'clock on Wednesday afternoon I was convinced the time had come! We prepared to take the eleven-mile journey to the hospital in Buffalo.

The sun was beginning to lower in the west on that May afternoon in 1951, and its warm spring rays touched the objects in our living room on Zurbrick Road in Depew, New York. I glanced around the unfinished parlor at the well-worn furniture and I was drawn, as so often before, to our upright piano, which stood on the east wall near the dining room.

With my outside wraps on, I sat down at the keyboard and softly played Stuart Hamblen's new song, "It Is No Secret What God Can Do." I sang, "What He's done for others, He'll do for you." I believed every word of it.

It had been an anxious road I had traveled the last few months. After all, I was thirty-nine, not exactly young anymore, and a mere four feet eleven inches tall. My husband, Charlie, six feet four inches tall, tried to conceal his concern for me. In my earlier deliveries my life had been in jeopardy. The outcome had been fine, however, and we have four healthy children.

David, the oldest, our six-foot muscular son, had been married for two years to the former Carol Kelly. They were the parents of two youngsters, David Jr. and Billy. Our brown-eyed, auburn-haired Nancy Jean was a senior at Depew High School. Janice, eleven, and Christine, four, were our lively blonds.

Contrary to the long hours of waiting on previous occasions, I went rather quickly into the delivery room. A little after 10:00 P.M. I was aware with a great wave of relief, that "it was all over."

A nurse moved back and forth across the room, her starched skirts swishing. Over to one side, not far from my cot, was a typical hospital crib. Two interns and a nurse were bending intently over it. Apparently my doctor had already disappeared.

"Is that my baby?" I eagerly questioned and, at the sound of my voice, they quickly scattered as if I had commanded them to do so. It startled me a little. The nurse who remained assured me that the baby was mine. "A little girl," she said, and cradled her in her arms for me to see.

"This is the ninth of May," I remembered. "My little girl has been born on my mother's birthday." Tears fell down my cheeks for love of the dear little mother whom I had known so briefly and for love of this new life entrusted to my care.

Then I spoke the name which Charlie and I had agreed would be hers: "Kathleen." "Kathleen Lucille," I repeated, "Kathy Lu." It sounded good! At last I could see her! It was all so wonderful! She looked like my other children, I decided, and I was satisfied.

The nurse gave me a speedy ride down the hall to the

room I would occupy for the next few days. A twenty-year-old mother, Mrs. Frank Gruber, delighting in the birth of her first child, was already there. We introduced ourselves and began getting acquainted. We were both too excited to sleep.

The next morning, as I lay waiting to be served my breakfast, I thought, "This is one of the happiest days of my life. I am all right. My baby is all right. Now we can plan for the future." Exhilarated, I joked with everyone. No one except my room-mate seemed to share my hilarity.

I heard the pleasant voice of our family physician as he greeted the nurses in the hall. Dr. C. is a general practitioner, and I have yet to see a doctor more dearly loved by hospital personnel than this man. He is of medium height, and he was bald when we first met him. He must have been in his early thirties at that time. Now, after almost twenty years, he was an important part of our lives, our friend as well as our physician.

There was a gravity about the doctor as he entered the room that I could not fathom. "Where were you last night when I awakened?" I chided, "why did you leave so soon?"

He avoided an answer, but, after inquiring how I was feeling, he said, "I think I shall have Dr. G. take a look at the baby today—just to be sure everything is all right." He was sober-faced and did not look directly at me.

I passed it off lightly. She looked fine to me. I had held her in my arms and checked to see if all of her fingers and toes were intact. Her eyes were closed, but she had a darling little round head and the funniest fold over her right ear. That was the nearest thing to a defect I had found.

The busy doctor was soon on his way, and I turned my attention to the slight, blonde nurse who was caring for me. She stood at the window, and seemed rather sad. My heart went out to her. "She has some trouble," I thought, all the while searching my mind for a comforting word for her.

A poem by Jane Merchant had appeared in the *Saturday Evening Post* a few weeks earlier. It was entitled: "Afterward." It had so impressed me that I memorized the words. I quoted it to her, ending with the words, "And hearts continue bearing the things they could not bear." I did not dream that her expression of pity was for me.

Charlie came in during visiting hours, still a bit tired from the worry of the night before. He looked handsome, as always, in his blue wool suit. His thinning brown hair still fell in a wave over his slanted forehead, and his boyish face belied middle age. He, too, was glad that we had reached this plateau. When he kissed me good-bye, he mentioned that he would stay at home with Chrissy and Janice that evening. Nancy had a date. That was all right, I assured him, for Kathy and I would be just fine.

I must have dozed awhile, for the clatter of trays in the hall startled me. Traffic was increasing outside the door, and Mrs. Gruber commented that supper must be on its way.

My tray was brought in and my bed cranked up so that I could enjoy eating in a sitting position. I had just peeked under the dish covers to see what was on the menu, when Dr. C. unexpectedly entered the room. I am sure that my face revealed my surprise.

He came over close to the bed and abruptly said, "I have bad news for you, Mrs. Schultz. Dr. G., the specialist, has examined your baby. He says she is Mongoloid."

I looked at him uncomprehendingly, and asked, "What does that mean?"

In a low voice he answered, "She has no mind!" And this dear family friend began to weep as he told me, "It is the first one I have delivered in my practice—and to think it had to happen to you!"

I felt the blood drain from my face. We are educated people. We had always been proud of our "good minds." Charlie had made excellent grades in school. My brothers are college men. Two of them are in the Christian ministry. If the diagnosis had been a physical disability, I could have understood, for I have had curvature of the spine and dislocated hips since birth. But mental trouble! It was a complete shock.

"What do people do in such circumstances?" I asked in a voice that sounded far off.

The doctor regained his composure and was businesslike again. "We advise that you place her in a Home," he told me. "If you take her home, she will be a blight to the other children. You must think of them, too. If you were caring for her, you might not recognize the fact that she is different until about five months had passed. Then you would see that she still did nothing. It would be much harder to give her up then." Then he added, "Please don't expect a miracle."

"I won't," I promised.

He seemed surprised that I had not cried out. All of the turmoil was within. He patted my arm and said, "You are a staunch soul, Mrs. Schultz."

I replied, "No, but I love the Lord with all my heart, and I know that he will never give me anything I cannot bear." I wondered, even then, if He had.

As the doctor left, he offered to call my husband and ask him to return to the hospital. I do not know yet why it was my task to give this sad information to Kathy's daddy, but perhaps it was better that way.

I noticed that Mrs. Gruber had listened to the conversation and was pitying me. I turned my head toward the window so that my tears could not be seen. My supper tray was forgotten. My mind whirled. I thought, "What will I tell Charlie?" He suffered from hypertension, and I feared the effect of this news on him.

When seven o'clock came, I heard the familiar stride in the hall. One glance at his face told me he knew nothing about the baby's affliction. He said briefly, "The doctor called and said you wanted something. Did you forget your curlers?" He eased himself into a chair. His very presence was comforting.

Hardly knowing how, I groped for words. "Did you ever hear of the word mongoloid?" I asked. He shook his head negatively. "Well," I continued, "it means 'no mind,' and Dr. C. says our Kathleen is like that!"

The shock was obvious on his face as he said, "That explains why he acted so strangely last night! He usually stops by to talk, but he waved and said, 'It's a girl, another Schultz,' and hurried out." Then, as the truth of the situation penetrated, Charlie was silent for a long time.

"What can we do?" he wanted to know. I told him all I knew. We agreed that we would not ask why. We would accept this seeming tragedy as from the hand of God.

We were not as brave as these words sound. It was pitiful, indeed, to see Kathy's father sit with his head in his hands as his world came shattering down around him. I did not help matters, either, for I became progressively more hysterical, begging him to take me home where I could pray in the quiet of my own room to try to find the will of God in the matter. I insisted that he call the doctor and ask permission for me to be released from the hospital. Frantically he tried to do this, but the doctor had wisely made himself unavailable. It was sink or swim, live or die, lose your mind or hang on to it!

CHAPTER 2

Beginning the "Road of Faith"

CHARLIE WALKED AWAY from the hospital in the spring night, unmindful of its beauty or of the scent of early blossoms. Mentally he was bewildered; physically he was nauseated. He had always taken his rightful place as the head of our household, assuming responsibility for its affairs. But, as he walked toward our car, his mind failed to find any solution to the present difficulty. Instinctively he lifted his heart, if not his voice, in prayer, and his mind groped for an answer.

The thought came to him rather suddenly as he drove out of the parking lot, that at least he had a clear conscience. He knew of no need for reprimand at the Lord's hand. He felt doubly glad that his conduct had been such that he did not need to blame himself for Kathy's condition.

It wasn't that he had lacked opportunity for misconduct. Perhaps this can be said of the entire human race, but in Charlie's case, the temptations had been rather explicit. He had been a member of the Buffalo Police Department since 1935, with all that this type of job entails. A few years later, he was promoted to the position of lieutenant. At the time of Kathy's birth Charlie headed the Anti-gambling Squad, working out of police headquarters.

As he drove south on Main Street he thought about the pressures that had come to bear upon him in his position—

various kinds of offers "just to look the other way," all of which he had refused. This was doubly important to him now, for he desperately needed God's help!

How he wished in this dark hour that he could go to his parents for guidance as to what to do. "Ma would understand," he thought, "for she lost three children out of nine!" But his parents were gone. Mr. Schultz died in 1941, and two years later Charlie's mother passed away. Kathy was born without a living grandparent, for my father had died in 1940.

We have a dear friend, Mrs. Vivian Root, who has "adopted" us as a part of her large family. I had known the Root family longer than I had known Charlie. Wally, Frances and Frank were my particular friends. Leslie, Whitman and Sarah were younger. When Mrs. Root met me the first time, and learned that I was a half-orphan, her generous heart went out to me in love, and from that time on I was "another daughter." I later learned that the Schultz family had lived across the street from the Roots at one time, and Wally and my husband Charlie had been friends. It was natural, on that night of sorrow when the world seemed upside down, for Charlie to go to Mrs. Root's home and tell her the tragic news.

When Charlie explained the doctor's report about our Kathy, quick tears of sympathy welled in the eyes of Mrs. Root and Frances as they realized the impact of this news on all of us. "I hated to have to tell you," Charlie went on, "but I knew you would want to know."

"Poor Edna," was all Mrs. Root could manage to say.

Thoughtful Frances asked who was cooking for Charlie and the family. He replied that everyone was taking a turn at it. She urged him to bring the girls for dinner on Sunday, and then he could visit me in the afternoon. He agreed to the plan.

Tired, almost to the point of collapse, Charlie drove home

and stumbled into the house. Nancy, Janice, and Chris were waiting to hear all about their new little sister. Their dad dismissed their questions and hurried to the sanctuary of our room where he could suffer without the eyes of anyone upon him.

The girls were puzzled. "What has happened to Daddy?" they asked, but none of them suspected the answer.

At the hospital I was struggling to keep my equilibrium. Throughout the midnight experience there was not one moment when I lost the consciousness of God's presence. As I sank deeper and deeper into the valley of despair, I knew beyond a doubt that this trial had come for a definite reason. I had no idea why, but I knew that we were not being punished for any past sins. As far as we knew, we were living consistently Christian lives. But we needed to find the will of God in this matter and to learn the lesson that He was trying to teach us.

After the hospital had quieted down and all visitors had left the building and most of the patients seemed to be sleeping, I reached for my New Testament, expecting to find some words of comfort. How many times the Word of God has been my refuge on a troubled sea! I was no stranger to its pages. As a child on a large farm in Indiana, I had heard my parents read from the Bible. They had loved it. In the intervening years I had committed many of its passages to memory. Through its messages God often had spoken to my heart.

I held the small book near to the light and turned at random to Matthew 9:35. These are the words which I read: "And Jesus went about all the cities and villages, teaching in their synagogues, and preaching the gospel of the kingdom, and healing every sickness and every disease among the people." My heart leaped at the word "healing." It had not occurred to me to pray for the healing of my little one. It was not that I didn't believe that God could heal. I had seen His hand in healing. It was just that I didn't want to "expect a miracle" as the doctor had said.

I remember praying, "Lord, are you giving me hope?" Then I shook my head and said, "Please, don't give me hope when there is no hope." I turned to the back of the book where the Psalms were included. "I won't find healing in the Psalms," I thought.

I was wrong. I turned to Psalm 30 and read, "O Lord my God, I cried unto thee, and thou hast healed me!" Then farther on I read, "Weeping may endure for a night, but joy cometh in the morning."

My heart leaped for joy! I began to really pray and ask the Lord if He would allow me to pray for healing for my little girl. Everywhere I turned in the Scriptures there were promises.

And so, haltingly and fearfully, yet trustingly, too, I stepped out on a road of faith. I could hardly wait for a new day to tell Charlie not to worry. The Lord had revealed to me that Kathy's mind would grow!

I knew, when the promise was made, that the Lord had given it to me only for her mental growth. I cannot tell how I knew this, but the Lord impressed me with it. I had no assurance of her physical well-being and had no guarantee that she would live, but I had the promise that as long as she lived she would be a joy.

It is not easy to walk on the faith road. Believe me, it is a thoroughfare where you walk alone, except for the One Who has given you the gift of faith. My words seemed as idle dreams to everyone else. "It is just a mother's wishful thinking for her child," many said.

The next morning, Dr. C. called, and as he left, he asked me what we intended to do about Kathy. "You should place your application as soon as possible," he added, "for it takes a little while to place a child in an institution."

"You have consulted with a specialist," I told him, "but

I am consulting with the Great Physician. We are going to take our baby home." He said no more. In all fairness to this fine man, I believe that he knew all along that we would do that very thing. He knew how much our children meant to us.

When Charlie came in, he found a great change in me. Since the night before I had become calm and composed. I told him about my experience with the Scriptures. He listened with a mixture of interest and skepticism. He had seen the Lord answer our prayers before, so it was not a new thought to him. But he found it hard to forget the doctor's words, "Don't expect a miracle." He did catch onto the ray of hope, however, and remarked, "We will certainly do all we can for her."

Sunday dinner at the Roots proved to be, as always, a delicious one. There was an air of gloom prevalent, though, as these dear friends so wholeheartedly shared our burden. Frances kept back her tears; she didn't want the girls to see her cry. Mrs. Root had received a lovely corsage of red rosebuds in honor of Mother's Day, and she selected three of the choice buds to send to me.

In her collection of antique dishes, there was a demitasse cup of a pale green tint, with a large hand-painted orchid on the side. Hurriedly she shoved the stems of the flowers into the dainty china cup and brokenly said, "Edna can do anything she wants to with the cup. The roses are because we love her."

I was enthusiastic about the cup when I saw it, for I have a collection of lovely ones. For a moment, I removed the buds, and in a quaint sacred ceremony, I raised the cup to eye level and said, "Do you see this cup? It will be a token between the Lord and us that He has promised us something. This will be Kathy's 'cup of promise.' "

The week there in the hospital was hard. At feeding time the nurses brought Kathleen to me and I gave her a bottle.

I had breast-fed my other children, but the doctor thought it would be best to give Kathy a formula. She was never hungry. I struggled with her for the whole feeding period, and managed to get her to take two and a half ounces. It was half an ounce more than any nurse could get her to drink! I cuddled her and loved her right away. She was such a little doll! Her little round face bore a resemblance to our other babies.

As I held her, I raised her up in a gesture of offering to the Lord and prayed, "Lord, I can take this baby home and give her the best of care, but I can't put within her that which is lacking. I have no healing in my hands. If she grows, it will be because of You." Then, perhaps, with a weakness of faith, I added, "If I am making a mistake, please take my baby to Thyself. Please, don't let me make a mistake."

One afternoon the Lord tested this prayer. I heard a voice over the loudspeaker in the hall, repeating again and again, "Calling Dr. C., calling Dr. C." Fear welled in my throat. "My baby is dead!" I turned my head away from my room-mate and, with tears streaming down my cheeks, prayed, "Lord, you know how much I wanted her, but Thy will be done."

I was mistaken! At the regular feeding time, Kathleen was wheeled into the room in her rattly little cradle. Oh, how I hugged her!

All week long I either sang or hummed, "It Is No Secret." As I sang snatches of it, Mrs. Gruber joined me with her rich alto voice. We heard no complaints from the other patients, but, now that I think of it, we didn't receive any singing contracts either!

Although the term "Mongoloid" had been new to me, I learned a great deal about it that week. I gathered a lot of information and misinformation. One tactful (?) person told me that these children are very grotesque. Her description of them was horrible. Several others who talked with me that week had known Mongoloid children, but in every case the reports of their growth were discouraging.

The Berean Sunday School Class of Prospect Avenue Baptist Church, Buffalo, where we are members, had announced Kathy's birth, and, not knowing the circumstances, many friends sent cards with congratulatory messages. After the truth was known, our friends worried about our reaction. Situations like that are inevitable.

There is usually quite a lot of traffic in the hospital halls. Besides the regular activity connected with the care of patients and the constant effort to keep the floors clean, there are happy couples on their way home with their latest offspring. Sometimes a young mother takes her constitutional by walking up and down the hall, up and down, with a peek into every room along the way.

One afternoon one of the exercisers dropped into our room to get acquainted. She had given birth to twins, and we were glad to hear all about them. She was a gay person and very talkative. She asked if we knew about the woman in the hospital who had given birth to a Mongoloid child. Halfway through the sentence, she realized that it was I. Her embarrassment was very evident, but I pretended not to notice.

Charlie, meanwhile, was having his own Gethsemane. He had not told the children what was wrong with Kathy Lu. They prepared meals for him, but he wasn't hungry. He came home from work and went immediately into the bedroom until it was time to visit me. They could only guess that all was not well.

When the day arrived that we were to take Kathy home, the nurse dressed her in the lovely little yellow nightgown that I had packed with such anticipation before she was born. Her skin was yellow also, because of a touch of jaundice. We even wrapped her in a yellow blanket, and she looked for all the world like a little Oriental. I vowed never to dress her in that color again, As she grew older, however, it was one of her better colors, accenting her beautiful yellow hair.

Charlie came into the room with some restraint. He was worried. Truthfully, we were both scared at this important step we were taking. After the birth of each of our other children, taking the baby home had been a joyous occasion. I was determined that this one would be, too. As I picked up Kathy from the hospital bed, I prayed, "Thank You, Lord. I believe that You have given me my baby." And we started for home in the car.

I was happy there were just the three of us—Kathy, her daddy, and me. I looked at her little dollface and her tiny hands. She looked beautiful, I thought. Her daddy also peeked at her. I think that it was on that ride that he fell in love with her. "She is cute," he agreed. "Real cute."

As we went into the house with the suitcase and Kathy Lu, the girls could hardly wait to see her. They all agreed that she was "beautiful."

I unpacked the bag. After the other things were put away, I unwrapped the fragile china cup. With a prayer that was almost a sob, I placed it on the top shelf of the china closet. There would be times ahead when I would need to be reminded of God's promise.

CHAPTER 3

A Measure of Peace—and Despair!

ZURBRICK ROAD was a side country lane for many years, skirting Cayuga Creek and dividing the village of Depew from the township of Cheektowaga. It was originally used as a wide path where cattle were herded along on their way to the stockyards in Buffalo. The road is scarcely a mile in length and connects Transit Road with less-traveled Bordon Road. It was named for the Zurbrick family who lived in the only house along its route, a place now owned by Mr. and Mrs. William Harrop.

We discovered the quiet lane almost simultaneously with several other people, and in 1940 we purchased two and a half acres of land on its south side, midway between its connecting thoroughfares. It was pasture land, about to be sold for back taxes, and had been used as public property, it seemed, for when we saw it a cow was staked out there for grazing, while people stopped along the road to gather in baskets the windfallen apples from the scraggly tree nearby.

After we bought the property, my methodical husband felt that the first move was to impress upon the minds of trespassers that the plot of ground was now privately owned. He posted signs to that effect, and began to plant trees and clear land with the enthusiasm of a new landlord.

In 1941 Charlie erected a 20′x26′ shell, built entirely of

used lumber, which we proudly called our "summer home." The day school closed in June, we packed our children, clothing, bedding, pots and pans into the car and gaily headed for a summer in the country.

This "moving" ceremony was repeated every summer until 1949, when we sold our small house on Hoyt Street in Buffalo and moved permanently into the somewhat improved summer home. I was not altogether happy with the move. I missed the handiness of city living. But, as we began to plan the enlargement of the home, I agreed to the change. In 1951, after two years of remodeling, I had to admit that the house was beginning to "shape up."

We still had much to do, but every year found us more comfortable. A twenty-foot living room had been added, yet unfinished, and there was the promise of a large bedroom over it. A cellar was completed under the new addition, and we expected eventually to have a gas furnace. In the meantime, we heated with an oil circulating stove.

It was to this home that we brought Kathy—frail, baby Kathy. It was not a pretentious place, but it was a home where there was enough love for all.

The news about Kathy's diagnosis spread quickly. "There is something wrong with the Schultz baby," people whispered.

Some of them came to see her. They filed in and out like people at a bier, silent, but inquisitive. And sympathetic. Everyone hoped that she would be all right, but none believed that she would. After all, "The doctor had said!"

I knew how Abraham of Bible times must have felt on his way to a new country. He knew not whither he went, but he knew with whom he walked. That was my situation. I did not know how the Lord intended to lead, but I had been assured that He would.

Satan actively opposes a life of faith. And, strangely enough, Christians sometimes are used unwittingly in this battle. When I tried to tell our friends that I believed the Lord was going to work in Kathy's life, I could see unbelief on their faces.

Children's Day in June was a time of special emphasis on youth in our church. It was also the day when babies and young children were dedicated to the Lord. This public demonstration was not necessary for us, for we had private-ly wholly dedicated our Kathleen to the Lord's will for her life. However, on the occasion of our Lord's baptism, He said to John the Baptist, "Thus it becometh us to fulfill all righteousness." Since the dedication of babies is the custom in our church, we wanted to be a part of the ceremony.

Kathleen was carefully dressed in new clothing that we had received at a lovely shower given before her birth. In fact, the shower was unique in that it was given for her father instead of for me, and he had the "privilege" of un-wrapping all of the presents. For her dedication, Kathy wore the green sweater and bonnet that had been the gift of our pastor's wife, Mrs. Winthrop Robinson. Kathy's face was already becoming round, and she looked so cunning with the green satin bow tied under her chin.

This was Kathy Lu's first trip to church. We hesitated to expose her to curious eyes, for it was natural for people to try to glimpse the Mongoloid baby. Our son David and his wife, Carol, with their second son, Billy, were at the same dedication.

It was a simple ceremony as parents and their children stood before the altar. However fervent were the prayers of the others, I doubt that they surpassed the fervency of the silent prayers we sent heavenward on that Sunday morning in behalf of the precious bundle in her daddy's arms. The other children were in various stages of noisiness, but our Kathy was quiet, as if listening to every word that Pastor Robinson said. It was a good day for all of us.

Laundry day was almost every day at our house. On the

following Wednesday I was hanging the damp things outside as usual. Our clothesline, filled with those inevitable
squares, revealed the fact that there was a baby in the house.
It was a sunny day, just right for drying. I was experiencing
a measure of rest, mentally, for nothing had happened thus
far to alarm us.

As I fastened the last clothespin in place, I heard the
faint tinkle of the telephone and dashed inside to answer it.
The voice I heard was a familiar one, but I was surprised
too, for the caller was one of my dearest older friends who
had moved to Chicago. She was passing through Buffalo
and "couldn't leave without calling."

She inquired as usual about each member of the family.
And, finally, "How is the new little girl?" My throat tight-
ened. I was getting sensitive about the question. But I
could not resent this dear one's concern. I replied that she
was doing very well.

She will never know how shocked I was at her next state-
ment. "I was afraid she was going to be like the little one
we knew about in Cleveland. That child lived thirteen years,
and all her life was spent lying almost lifeless in the crib.
She never spoke!"

I was suddenly weak. I held on to the phone for dear
life. I managed to control my voice until good-byes were
said, but I found that I could hardly walk, I was so frightened. The impact of the words almost overwhelmed me.
But not quite.

I fled to our bedroom and threw myself onto my knees by
the bed. In utter helplessness I cried, "Oh, God. Don't let
my baby be like that! I couldn't bear it!" And then I remembered again, "Weeping may endure for a night, but
joy cometh in the morning."

"Dear God," I prayed again, "You will keep Your word.
It is Your word against man's word." And I was supernatur-
ally comforted.

CHAPTER 4

Lessons in Patience

WHEN MY OTHER CHILDREN were babies, I had taken for granted their normal development. Of course they smiled! Didn't all babies smile? Naturally they cooed. They noticed things. And later, they reached for toys, sat up, walked, and talked. I expected them to. There was no problem. I did not lose an hour's sleep worrying about what they would do or not do tomorrow.

Not so with Kathy. I obtained a New York State baby book, and it became my guide. I thumbed through its pages daily to read again what a baby should do at two weeks, three, a month, two months. I studied Kathy just as carefully.

Bath time was fun time for Kathleen and me. I sponge-bathed her most of the time, and as she lay on the padded table, even in the first month of her life, she was active. She would raise her wobbly head and wiggle her slippery body, almost getting away from my soapy hands. She enjoyed the rubdown with oil, and having powder smoothed on her skin.

I could see that she was gaining in weight—not at the same rate as her brother and sisters had, but gaining anyway. She screwed her little face into a crooked smile, right on time, and there was no doubt that she was aware of her surroundings.

After her bath, I would pick her up in her fresh-smelling clothes, and she snuggled her head into the hollow of my neck as if to say, "I love you, too!"

I learned new lessons in patience every feeding time. Kathy wasn't hungry. Never, never, never. It was a bother to her to be forced to eat. Force her, I did, determinedly removing the nipple from her bottle and spoon-feeding the milk to her. She had to swallow it!

Kathy never cried. I think she was a month old before she gave even a little holler. Then, one Sunday afternoon, she found her voice, and yelled in a sort of falsetto all afternoon. I don't know why it made us so frantic. I know now that it was a very good sign. At the time, we thought something was radically wrong. We took her up and down Zurbrick Road in the buggy until she finally hushed and went to sleep.

I kept Kathy Lu in her buggy near me during the daytime. At night she slept in the sturdy white wooden crib which had belonged to each of the other children in turn. I would look at her in the buggy over and over again, mentally urging her to show development which was far beyond her age.

One morning she was moving her hands around aimlessly, when she happened to touch the side of the buggy. Then, she deliberately touched it again. I was wild with joy! It was a clear sign of her awareness and progress!

It hadn't taken Kathy long to wrap her devoted father around that short little finger which "didn't quite reach the first joint of the ring finger." (That was supposed to be one indication of mongolism. Also, the straight line across her left hand which is known in medical circles as the simian fold.) Charlie saw to it that his new little daughter was always comfortable. He provided vitamins and special concoctions recommended by the doctor to increase her appetite. In his effort to spoil Kathy he was assisted by her sisters, who cuddled and petted her like a cherished doll.

Still, almost every conversation with people brought us discouragement. "She will develop just so far," they would tell us with authority, "and then she will level off."

I would go back again to the promises on which I had first rested, or walk in the light of a new one. I found them everywhere. I needed them so. They came in my private reading of the Bible. I heard them in the pastor's sermons. And once, when I was sorely afraid, I found fresh strength in words spoken during a wedding ceremony.

Charlie and I were invited to attend the wedding of a young man whom we had known since he was a small boy. We knew that we were expected to attend, but in our circumstances, we did not feel particularly gay. We decided to go just for the ceremony and return home.

As the pastor gave a sermonette in connection with the marriage rite, he quoted a verse that I had forgotten for the moment. It was Romans 8:28. "And we know that all things work together for good to them that love God, to them who are the called according to his purpose." *How could I have forgotten that?* I wondered. *Of course, this would work together for good!*

Kathy was three months old. So far, so good. The Lord had kept His promise thus far. She was a real joy to us. It was wonderful to have a baby in the house again. She was beginning to hang onto her rattle, and she enjoyed the activity that always has been charactertistic of our home.

A photographer came through our neighborhood one day, and we dressed our little doll in a soft silk dress for her first picture. There had been earlier snapshots, but this one would be posed! When the photographer later came with four poses of her, we did not hesitate. We bought every one!

In the arms of her adoring father, Kathy began to attend church. There he checked the air condition of the nursery, and otherwise made a nuisance of himself to those in charge. He wasn't going to leave Kathy any place that wasn't just right for her! If she so much as whimpered, he was right there to take her out into the other part of the church where she could be more comfortable. It didn't take her long to "catch on," and the two of them together in some corner, obviously enjoying each other's company, became a familiar sight.

As the weeks went by, our neighbors became accustomed to the sight of a large man wheeling the tiny little girl down the road in her buggy. Later the buggy was replaced by a red wagon. As Charlie strolled along, the neighbors used to run out to the road to see Kathy and to observe how well she was developing. They were sharing our burden, as good neighbors do.

Mrs. Jesse Kivett, our next-door neighbor, dropped in for a cup of coffee with me one morning. She is one of those people who are so nice to know — always there when needed, but too busy to be overfriendly.

She remarked that it puzzled her how I could continue our pattern of living as if nothing had happened. "If I had been told such discouraging news concerning one of my children, I think I would have stayed right at home. I wouldn't have had the heart to keep going," she told me. I am sure she would have been as brave as she thought I was.

I answered, "Don't you see? That is the only way I can go on. If I didn't get the spiritual food each Sunday from the pastor's sermons, I would soon go down in despair while waiting for Kathy to develop. It is imperative for me to go to church. I think I would die otherwise."

I looked into my clothes closet one day and realized that my wardrobe needed replenishing. This called for a shopping expedition! Kathy would have the best baby-sitter in the world, her father. I had a charge account and well-filled purse, so I sallied forth with a warning from you-know-who that I didn't have to spend it all in one day. It was a short walk to the bus, and in no time I was in the stores, looking at price tags and comparing materials like a seasoned shopper.

One of the clerks in the department store was rather talkative. As she assisted me in making my purchases, I told her that I had recently given birth to my fifth child. "I really need to replenish my wardrobe," I admitted.

"Well, if you have healthy children, be thankful," she said. And then, "There is a family in our neighborhood who had three wonderful youngsters, and then they had a Mongolian idiot!"

She was too busy to notice how that remark affected me. I was numb again, a feeling that I was becoming familiar with. In what I hoped was an offhand manner, I asked, "What has become of the Mongoloid child?"

"Oh, he is about eighteen years old now," she explained, "and he hangs around the street. Of course, he doesn't know anything," she added. She could not have cut me more if she had physically stabbed me with a knife!

As I boarded the bus for Depew, there was a full moon. I tried to compose myself and enjoy the scenery, which was unusually beautiful that bright summer night. I couldn't ignore the pounding of my heart, which pained me with each beat. The other passengers could not hear my wild inward cry, but I knew God heard it, as I repeated again, "It is Your word against man's word."

Life has a way of going on, despite the stormy winds or roar of the sea, and I soon gained my composure again. We could not deny that Kathy was frail. She frequently had colds and lung congestion. Through it all, she was a happy baby. And not in the least grotesque!

I seemed to have the capacity to go along fine for a while, and then I would begin to worry. Again and again I could hear the words of the specialist, "She has no mind." By the time she was six months old, there was no doubt that she did have a mind. The next problem was to find out how much use she could make of it. I found myself putting her through tests. It was so hard for me to wait. I wanted to see!

One day I remembered that my other children had been able to sit alone at six months of age. The thought electrified me! Kathy had not accomplished that yet. I decided that it was time for her to sit up. Although it was obvious that she was not ready for that adventure, I sat her on the floor and piled pillows all around to break her fall. I was going to teach her to sit alone!

For about a half hour, I tried to teach her to balance herself. As the minutes passed, both of us became more and more frustrated. I would set her up, and she would fall over. Finally I recognized how frayed my nerves were. Looking at the tear-stained face of my baby, I felt ashamed of myself. I ceased from my frantic efforts and accepted her just as she was. I promised her and the Lord that I would be willing to wait until she was ready to sit alone. At eight months she fulfilled my wish for her without difficulty.

We were all so happy that Kathy was able to sit alone, especially her daddy. He bragged about it to anyone who would listen. Among those who listened was a man who was the father of a severely retarded child. He commented, "If your child can sit up at the age of eight months, get down and kiss the ground!" His poor little girl had waited two years to advance that far.

CHAPTER 5

"Are You Willing for Her Not to Develop as You Expect?"

THREE PICTURES had been placed in Kathleen's album: her first picture, taken at three months, a smiling pose at six months, and a third picture, taken a few days before her first birthday, which showed her sitting on a table, her chubby legs primly folded beneath her.

On the actual anniversary of her birth, Kathy's sisters were in school, but her father and I decided to declare a holiday and take Kathy for a ride. With sandwiches, canned baby food and milk packed in a handy box, we drove to Batavia to visit Clarence and Bertha Madill, old and valued friends of ours.

Bertha and I were kindred spirits. She was an earnest Christian, and she had had lots of trouble. Her baby Crystal had been born with an enlarged head. After four months the little one died. The Madills had experienced other family tragedies which made them very warm and sympathetic to the burdens of others.

During our visit with them, Bertha broached the subject of Kathy's future. I repeated the promises that I was sure were mine from God's Word. She nodded at mention of the Scriptures, then, kindly but seriously she asked the question, "Would you be willing for Kathy's development not to be as you expect?"

Her query startled me and for a moment I floundered. Then, stalwartly I replied, "No, I am not willing! I was willing for God's will in the first place when I thought Kathy would not develop. Then, He showed me that He would intervene. I cannot do otherwise but believe He will keep His word. She *has* to develop."

I had learned to be stubborn about this subject. I could not expect that other Christians would be able to believe with me. God had not given them the gift of faith to believe for my circumstance. Nor could I always believe for them as they rested on certain promises. God had definitely given me faith for my need, and I was exercising it.

Kathy loved the fuss we made that evening as we sang "happy birthday" to her. We were home in time for supper and her sisters slyly helped blow out the candles on the heart-shaped cake. She sat smugly in her high chair like a little queen. There were presents, too, which Christine helped her to open. Her vocabulary was limited, but her squeals of delight told us how happy she was with each gift.

Since Kathy's birth our lives had of necessity revolved around her. However, there were occasions when celebrations were in order for other members of the family. Janice had graduated from sixth grade. Another grandchild had been born and was named Kelly Schultz. (What a lot of fighting he will have to do over that name! At least, that's what our German relatives predicted.) Charlie was receiving complimentary editorials from the Buffalo papers for his fine work on the squad. And there was Nancy's high-school graduation.

Charlie's sister, Anna Hornung, stayed with Kathy at our home while we attended the graduation exercises. We proudly watched our daughter accept her music award and regents' diploma. Later, other members of the family joined us for a party at our house. Raymond Morningstar, who had graduated from Depew the year before, was also invited to the celebration with his parents. Ray had been Nancy's steady date during high school, and was then enrolled at Buffalo State Teachers College.

We all liked Ray. He was a tall, quiet young man, clean-cut and unassuming. It was refreshing to meet one who was not so insecure that he had to "follow the crowd." He was a member of St. John's Lutheran Church in Depew, and our conniving daughter often attended social events promoted by the Lutheran young people. Her motives were ulterior, I have no doubt. I can now report that her conniving worked! A couple of years later, Nancy and Ray were married.

After working during the summer, Nancy entered Providence Bible School in the fall. We visited her there several times, and she came home for Christmas. Then it was March and time for spring vacation.

On the Friday night that Nancy arrived at home, Kathy developed a heavy cold. By Sunday afternoon, she was breathing so laboriously that we called an emergency doctor who ordered her to the hospital. We were referred to Dr. W., a pediatrician. He became especially interested in his patient when he noted the Mongoloid characteristics. He busily took notes on her general appearance and ordered treatment for her. He looked up from his writing to say, "Of course, you realize that this child is Mongoloid?"

I assured him that we had been informed of her condition. Apparently there was something in the way I answered that annoyed him. "You do not seem to take this fact very seriously." He was impatient.

Wearily, as I had done so many times before, I replied, "Dr. W., no *man* can tell how far our child will develop. We are taking this a day at a time with prayer."

"But you cannot ignore facts," he said curtly.

We engaged a private room for Kathy, and a cot was placed in it for my convenience. I could not leave her alone.

I wanted to be nearby to reassure her, and to do for her what was needed. We settled down for our stay, I with a heavy heart, she with bronchial pneumonia. She was placed under oxygen and a course of treatment was begun.

Our family doctor was in constant touch with us, but he advised us to place Kathy in the care of a child specialist. Reports could be sent to him as they were given.

After two weary days, the doctor told us, "I suspect a heart condition. You will notice that her chest is rather bulged. I think we will take a picture to see what causes the fullness."

Kathy was tired of her oxygen tent by this time, and welcomed a ride down the hall to the elevator and up to the Xray department. I walked beside her as the nurse pushed the wheel chair. "Everything will be all right," I assured her.

What an interesting but sad place the Xray department is! There I saw people with all types of ailments waiting their turn. Some of the cases were so pitiful I quickly looked away to avoid staring. And others looked at us.

When Kathy saw the Xray equipment, she began to scream. I remembered when I had first been introduced to such machinery the fear that I had felt — in Frankfort, Indiana, when I was eight years old. Kathy continued to howl while I held the film to her chest. When it was all over, she couldn't believe she hadn't actually been hurt!

The report confirmed Dr. W.'s fears. Kathy's heart was gross and very defective. I was stunned as I listened to the bad news. *We have had her for twenty-two months,* I thought, *and how precious she is to us!* It was a man-sized blow to Charlie.

We continued the day-and-night vigil by Kathy's crib, but she did not improve. Again, Dr. W. conferred with me. "I have bad news for you," he said. I could see that it was difficult for him to tell me. "Kathy is not going to live. Her blood has overflowed her heart, and she will probably pass away within the next twenty-four hours."

I was alone when the doctor revealed this shocking development to me. I had been alone when I first learned that she was Mongoloid. But, I was not really alone. The presence of the Lord was very real to me and I was able to accept this, too, as from Him. The hardest part was to repeat to Kathy's adoring daddy, for she was truly his sunshine.

After work Charlie came to the hospital. His face was drawn with worry as he took Kathy's little hand in his large one. He kissed the fingers, one by one. The tender scene was almost too much for me, as, for the second time in Kathy's brief life, I told her father that the doctor considered her case hopeless. "She is going to die," I said softly.

Again, as on that first occasion, Charlie placed his head in his hands in a gesture of agony. I shall always remember what he said, "If I could just take her home again, and pull her in the wagon down the road a couple of more times, I would be happy."

With death imminent, Charlie insisted on staying right in the hospital with Kathy, and we took turns watching by her crib. One of us slept while the other watched.

Kathy loved to have me sing to her. (I had at last found someone who appreciated my talent!) One of our favorites was: "Jesus, Saviour, Pilot Me," especially the verse that says, "As a mother stills her child, Thou canst hush the ocean wild." For that particular occasion, one song seemed to fill my need. The words are:

> Neighbors are kind, I love them everyone.
>   We get along with sweet accord,
> But when my soul needs manna from above,
>   Where could I go but to the Lord?*

---

* These lines from the song "Where Could I Go?" copyright 1940, published in GOLDEN KEY, are used by kind permission of Stamps-Baxter Music and Printing Co.

As the hours went by, I had plenty of time to think. We had been pleased at the mental progress Kathleen had made. She was beginning to talk, saying the usual Daddy and Mama, and a few other words. In many ways she was developing normally, while in others she was decidedly slow. She was still unable to walk. Her first tooth appeared at fourteen months of age. After that, the others came in rather rapidly. They were nice straight healthy-looking teeth, too. Kathy Lu was rather roly-poly, no longer pale, but with nice rosy cheeks. Her hair was her most beautiful gift. It was golden in color, and of a silken texture. What she lacked in oral expression, she made up in love. Even Chrissy, who was such a little girl herself, did not consider Kathy a competitor, but rather her darling little sister.

We were fortunate that Nancy was at home for two weeks to take care of the others. It gave us opportunity to devote our entire time to this little one who needed us so.

We talked together about the funeral plans. Of course, we would have her at home. We couldn't bear not to. Nancy and Aunt Anna began to get the house ready.

Since childhood I had dabbled in writing poetry, and as I sat there, I composed several poems about Kathy's passing. Charlie knew what I was writing, but he did not ask to see my poems. Nor did I offer to let him read what I had written. He was too crushed. Once, when he had gone out for lunch, he noticed a child down the hall who was being taken home by its parents. When he returned, he told me, "Some day, maybe in a year or two, I want you to write a poem for me. Write it about the ones who don't go home," and he choked with grief. This was the only poem Charlie had ever requested, and it never was written.

CHAPTER 6

"A Light Appeared"

I HAD LOST all conception of time. I only knew that another day had slipped away and night had come. It was my turn to watch by the crib. We expected our little one to die at any time, and Charlie was resting for a few minutes in preparation for duty the rest of the night. The hospital was quiet, and the room was dimly lit by the light from the hall, beyond the partly closed door.

As I watched, I suddenly realized that a light was shining on Kathy's crib. I thought, "Someone has turned on a light!" Then I looked in the direction from which it came, and saw that the window was as dark as could be. The light seemed to come from the corner ceiling of the room.

Then I thought, "This cannot be! This must be my imagination!" Then an afterthought came, "If there is really a light, there will have to be a shadow."

I slowly arose and stepped over to the crib. As I held my hand above Kathy, there was a distinct shadow! Mechanically I sat down again, still wondering. It seemed to me that the door of Heaven had opened just a bit and heavenly light had come streaming through! The light was not penetrating like sunlight but rather like the glow of the moon. "It is as if they are watching us and want us to know that we are not alone," I decided.

I did not know when the light disappeared. It had appeared subtly, and was removed in the same way.

39

Since I first became a Christian in my twentieth year, I have tried to measure every spiritual experience by the Word of God. What could be the intended message for me? In my excitement, the only verse of Scripture I could think of was: "Satan himself is transformed into an angel of light." I knew that this was not God's message to me, but I was not sure what the true message was.

I am not a person who periodically "sees visions." I have needed no supernatural manifestation to tell me of God's love through the years. I wanted to be counted among those spoken of by St. Peter, who having not seen Christ yet loved Him. But a vision had come. How could I explain it to Charlie?

I needn't have worried. He awakened shortly afterward, and I told him the story. He needed no convincing; he knew it was real to me. I prayed that he would see the light, too, but he did not. It was evidently God's exclusive dealing with me.

For my devotions the next morning, I read the first chapter of John in the New Testament. It was a familiar portion of Scripture. In fact, I had memorized it some years before. On this particular day, the words fairly leaped from the page. Here was my explanation! "In him was life," I read, "and the life was the light of men. And the light shineth in darkness; and the darkness comprehendeth it not." I began to see. The light was a sign to us that Kathy would have life!

Our pastor, the Rev. Winthrop Robinson, visited the hospital soon after the vision had occurred, and I hesitantly told him my experience. He informed me that the Scripture portion can be read, "The light shineth in darkness and the darkness cannot put it out!"

I did not mention this unusual event to many people. I felt a little like St. Paul must have when he said, "I . . . heard unspeakable words not lawful for a man to utter."

I realized that to tell many people would be to "cast . . . pearls before swine." Most people would neither believe nor understand. Kathy's story would not be complete, however, if this supernatural experience were not included.

Doctors and nurses agreed that Kathy would die. The next night their predictions seemed to be coming true. Her temperature, which had been about 102, began to drop. Down it went, past the normal 98 to 96, on to 94, and finally to 92. The nurse piled covers on Kathy to try to keep warmth in her body. Miraculously, her temperature began to climb again and was soon normal. She continued to live!

I stayed by Kathy's crib, even refusing to leave for food. Charlie supplied that for me on paper plates from time to time. One morning when he brought bacon, eggs, and toast on a plate, Kathy raised herself up from her pillow and wanted some! It was her first interest in food, and I gladly shared my breakfast with her. We could see that she was feeling better. A week passed, and she steadily improved.

While we had kept the vigil at the hospital, the congregation at Prospect Church had prayed faithfully for Kathy. Pastor Robinson called regularly, and one night when Kathy's condition was most critical, he stayed long into the night, giving us his spiritual support. The good news of Kathy's improvement spread quickly, and everyone rejoiced with us.

By this time, Dr. W. was puzzled. He admitted that he did not know how she could continue to live. But she did. In answer to our question about taking Kathleen home, the doctor told us that it would be precarious. "She might live a month, but certainly not much longer," he predicted.

We talked and prayed together about what we should do. Then we decided to take her home. Arrangements were made for an oxygen tank to be placed in our bedroom, and one happy day we turned onto Zurbrick Road on our way home!

What rejoicing there was in our household! Instead of having a funeral, we brought home a very-much-alive little girl! We were aware that the road ahead would be a rough one as we continued the battle for her life. We were now conscious of Kathy's defective heart.

Nancy left for Providence Bible School the next morning. Her spring vacation had not been a happy one, but she was relieved that her little sister was so much better.

We settled down to the business of nursing Kathy back to health.

CHAPTER 7

The Promised Joy Becomes Reality

AFTER WE DISCOVERED Kathy's heart condition, we entered into a new phase in our care of her. Instead of watching for signs of her mental development, we were concerned, for the most part, about the possibility of heart failure. Her primary problem was a physical one. We were told that it was all-important for her to avoid contact with any viruses, because her particular enemy was bronchial trouble.

We lived as normally as possible under the circumstances. We entertained guests often, as did our children. We found that it was necessary to carefully screen visitors for any sign of colds. It could mean life or death to Kathy.

Our friends cooperated beautifully. They stayed away when they were ill. The children's friends became used to "the third degree" at the door, and disciplined themselves in the matter. "I can't go to Schultzes today," they would say. "I have to wait till I'm over this cough!"

Charlie and I found that our days and nights were pretty much the same during this period of Kathy's life. We slept when we could. We poured oxygen into her lungs to relieve her labored breathing. She was receiving Digiten twice daily. We guarded her from any undue excitement or strain. It was a strenuous battle.

After a final catnap before the alarm rang, I would open

one eye, squint at Charlie, and ask, "Do you think we'll make it today?"

"Oh, sure," he would answer with a yawn.

The girls were simply wonderful. Christine ran untold numbers of errands for me. Janice learned to operate the washing machine, and after school she tackled the weekly laundry. Nancy returned from college in June and started to work for the Loblaw Company in Buffalo. The girls helped with the housework. They prayed, too. All were in complete agreement that we must bring Kathy through, at all costs.

Color began to return to Kathy's cheeks. She began to breathe easier, and so did we. She took an active interest in using her legs. She walked around the furniture, or held onto our hands for support. She was a determined little peanut, and although she fell again and again, she was more determined than ever to master the art of walking. She had plenty of "get up and go" if she could just get going!

It was a pleasant summer. "Grandma" Root and Frances came out for a picnic in July. "I'm glad Kathy is little," Mrs. Root remarked, as she watched the tyke balancing herself on her sturdy but unsure legs. "All of your children are growing so tall like Charlie, but Kathy is small like you."

Charlie built a sandbox east of the house under the wild cherry tree, where there was plenty of shade. Then he and Kathy shopped at Murphy's five-and-dime store where they bought a bright red pail and a light shovel. After that, Kathy spent hours building sand houses and digging sandy tunnels. Christine aided and abetted the construction by carrying water from the house. The results were sloppy but entertaining.

Sometimes Chrissy seated herself in the swing, with Kathy on her lap, and they would soar together "up in the wild blue yonder." The higher they swung, the more delighted Kathy was.

Janice would snatch her little sister up into her arms and the two of them would wheel away on the bike if our backs were turned. Janice thought that hearing Kathy's gleeful squeals was worth the scolding she would get for "double riding."

As for Dad, the wish he had expressed at the hospital to "take her down the road once more" was fulfilled a hundred times over. Every evening, after supper, they disappeared out the driveway, with Dad the "horse" and Kathy the driver in the wagon.

Although there were but few houses on Zurbrick Road when we bought our land, since that time many new homes had been built. If Charlie and Kathy turned to the left, they greeted the Kivetts who were usually working in their yard. Then, on to Groves, whose lawn is like a formal garden. Frank Groves works for a tree-trimming company, and he spends his spare time improving his own land. Farther down the road, they came to the Lawsons and Jakubowskis. Usually by this time, Chris had caught up on her bike, and even Janice had joined the walk. Mrs. Lawson, a tender-hearted woman who particularly loves children, always ran out when she saw the red wagon rolling along. She had to have a "little talk with Kathy."

If the "horse" and wagon headed east, there were the Stichts, Grannises, Tromburgs, and Harrops to greet. Billy Harrop, Junior, who was getting training to teach retarded children, was very interested in Kathy. "I don't think she is retarded," he told his mother. "See how she remembers our names from one visit to the next!"

Candy Mahaney lives farther down the road. Candy was about Kathy's age, and they were good friends. It was a common sight as they grew older to see Candy coming to our door with a book or some crayons for her friend, Kathy.

Only mothers like myself, who have had an "exceptional" child, can appreciate how much it means to have other children show kindness to the little one "with the broken wing." Neighborhood children can be very cruel. This condition can be remedied by parents, who should admonish their youngsters to be particularly kind to the weaker ones. Such parents merit the lifelong appreciation of people like myself who are raising a defective child. We had no problem in our neighborhood. Every child treated Kathy with the greatest kindness.

The time was approaching for a family gathering of the Moore clan. My parents, Mr. and Mrs. Emerson E. Moore, had six children. Norris H., Alvin C., Emil J., myself, Walter E., and Burton F. Except for Walter, who died in infancy, we were brought up on a farm in Monroe County, Indiana. As the years passed we were scattered in all directions. Because of this, when we gathered at the funeral of my father, Norris suggested that we make a covenant that when any one of us became fifty years of age, the others would meet with that one for a celebration. "We ought to meet for a joyous occasion instead of only when there is a death in the family," he reasoned. We all agreed.

The first celebration had taken place before Kathy's birth, but in November of 1953, Alvin was reaching the half-century mark.. He lived on the farm where we were raised. I was reluctant to go, since it was impossible to take Kathleen on a 600-mile trip and I had not left her since her birth.

I prayed very definitely about my decision. I asked the Lord to show me in some way that I should stay at home if it was not His will for me to go. I fully expected to develop a fever or find that one of the children had come down with measles, but nothing of the sort happened. Everything fell into place for the trip, so I committed Kathy to the Lord and went. Her father was more than happy to take a week of his vacation and spend the time with her!

It is imperative for mothers with problems such as mine to get away from the stress for a season. No woman should feel guilty because she has taken a little time away from her family, if she can be sure that they will be well taken care of.

I must confess that I did not go lightheartedly, but I did trust the Lord. The God we serve is not cruel, and I knew that He would not give me more than I could bear. If Kathy had passed away during my absence, it would have been unbearable!

Our reunion was all that we could have wished for. Norris, the owner of a chain of Moore's Fiesta Restaurants, was there. As usual, he was "bossing the rest of us around," which is the prerogative of a "big brother." His family accompanied him; they included his wife Lucille, his sons, Harold and Loren, and their wives, Irene and Phyllis. Alvin was gay, with all of the attention focused on him. His wife Marguerite was the soul of hospitality. Emil, a minister in the Christian Church in Tucumcari, New Mexico, came with his wife, Lottie. And "little brother Burt," then the pastor of the Baptist Church at Campbellsport, Wisconsin, was on hand, too. His wife Dorothy had stayed at home with the four children, Kathleen, Jerald, Emerson, and Linda. Alvin's boys were cavorting all around the place — Duane, Larry and Michael — each vying for attention.

All in our family enjoy the same hobbies. We play musical instruments, mostly by ear, and we made the countryside ring that week. We even harmonized on the old favorites. What difference did it make if we slid into the notes? We finally made it!

Of course, we all like good food. There was an abundance of that.

I reassured myself concerning Kathy with a telephone call

to Charlie in the middle of the week, and he told me every-thing was "under control."

Then, it was over. We scattered by car and train back to our homes. I was happy indeed to be greeted at the railroad station not only by Charlie but by Chrissy and Kathy, too.

Kathy still did not express herself fully, but she hugged and hugged me all the way home, and I knew she was very glad to see "Mama" again.

After I had hung my traveling clothes in the closet, Charlie and I sat at the kitchen table to enjoy a cup of coffee and to catch up on the news. Suddenly, I heard one of the sweetest sounds that had ever reached my ears! Little feet were pitter-pattering from the living room out to the kitchen! Rounding the corner, Kathy's little pixie face lighted as she came toddling to my chair. She could walk!

I grabbed her to me and squeezed her until she squealed. I was overjoyed! She could walk! She could walk! I danced around the kitchen with her in my arms. "Oh, God," I breathed, "thank You! Thank You!"

With this plateau reached, it was a series of wonderful things. A new world opened to our Kathleen. She investi-gated, played, examined everything in sight, and became a busy, busy little person.

A friend of ours from Prospect had been interested in Kathy's progress since her birth because a Mongoloid child had been born to our friend's sister. We compared notes many times. The niece was in constant motion when she slept, but lay perfectly still when she was awake.

I had to admit that Kathy was a restless sleeper. (Later we attributed it partly to the heart condition.) But Kathy was not motionless when awake. Far from it! And with the newly acquired locomotion, she found many new delights in a day's time.

"Our Betsy never played with a doll in her life," our friend had said. "She just wasn't interested." It was by these comparisons that I knew Kathy was making substantial progress.

When one starts with the idea that a child will do nothing, as we did, every step forward is hailed by a celebration. We were experiencing daily joys as we observed her interest in everything around her. The "joy in the morning" had become a reality.

CHAPTER 8

Cold Fear—but God is Near

AT ABOUT THE TIME Kathy learned to walk she began to put words together. Chrissy had been "Kiki" to her for a long time, and "Shashy" was as near as she could come to saying "Janice." We could understand many of the words she tried, but actual sentences seemed to be beyond her reach.

When Kathy napped in the afternoon, I would lie beside her for a while and read simple Bible stories. I felt that this child was only loaned to us, and it was important for her to know about the Lord Jesus. I would say to her, "Kathy, Jesus loves you."

One day, we went through the usual procedure. I closed the book and remarked, "Jesus loves you." She brightened expressively, and, with her closed fist, she pounded her chest. "Jesus, me!" she said with a surprised look.

After that, she began to couple words, sometimes incongruously, but we loved to hear her baby voice saying them. Her "Daddy-Piggy" couplet tickled her sisters, who wouldn't quite dare to say such a thing!

People watched Kathy's progress with much interest. Pity for us had been replaced by surprise at Kathy's accomplishments. One day, a Lancaster friend stopped by. She watched Kathy for a while as she played about the room. Then the lady told me, "I once had a cousin who was Mongoloid. My

aunt devoted her life to taking care of her invalid daughter.
The girl lived to be about twenty-five years old but never
grew beyond the stage of creeping about the floor. Kathy's
progress is a real miracle."

Some people were unsympathetic, but they were in the
minority. We heard about them indirectly. One young
woman, immature, to say the least, remarked, "If I had a
child like Kathy, I wouldn't pour oxygen into that life as
they are doing." She felt it would be more merciful to let
the Lord take the child without a struggle. (Kathy's daddy
marked that girl off his "Christmas list" right away!)

Then there were the kindhearted, generous-minded people
like Kenneth and Nancy Hains. I saw Nancy for the first
time when she walked down the aisle of Prospect Avenue
Baptist Church at a Sunday morning worship service. Coming in late, she was breathless, and beautiful. Following her
was Kenneth, looking the part of the successful business
man, which he was. He was of medium height, blond with
thinning hair, and his blue eyes scanned the congregation
as he walked along. Nancy's dark beauty was startling. I
learned later that she was born of an Irish mother and
Roumanian father. Her heritage from them had combined
to form a lovely person, both in looks and in manner.

I made a mental note to speak to these strangers after the
service. I learned that day that Mr. and Mrs. Hains were
living in Lancaster, a twin city of Depew, so we were neighbors. Later, we got to know the couple very well.

They particularly admired our Christine, who was a
chubby, blond three-year-old at the time. They were child-
less, and longed for a little girl "just like Chrissy." A couple
of years later they adopted Priscilla, who greatly resembles
our daughter. Since that time, they have been blessed with
a second child.

We often were entertained in the Hains' home. They
would invite visiting missionaries and Prospect members

to their home on Sunday evenings after the worship services. Sometimes it was just our family who enjoyed the Hains' hospitality.

One such occasion stands out clearly in my mind. It was one of Kathy's "red letter" days. We sat at the table enjoying our coffee after the delicious meal. Kathy had climbed on my lap, and was quietly listening to the grown-up conversation. Then, perhaps to gain my attention, she looked at me and distinctly said, "I love Mommy!" It was her first complete sentence.

Then, it was a game. "I love Mommy." "I love Daddy." "I love Kiki." "I love Shashy." We were thrilled, for we knew that if she could say these sentences, she would soon say many others. We had learned that the things that other children were "born knowing," Kathy had to be taught. These things did not come to her easily, but they did eventually come!

Kathleen lived precariously. We tried to tuck the knowledge of her heart condition back in the recesses of our minds. We smiled and worked and joked . . . and worried. We tried not to admit it. We spoke optimistically, but we did not fool one another for a moment. She had grown into a darling-looking little girl, and we certainly did not want to lose her.

Every good detective story has the expression "cold fear" somewhere within its framework. If it adequately describes situations that are the figment of the author's imagination, how much more it pinpoints the feelings we had in facing the reality of Kathy's condition.

By day her breathing was not audible, and we relaxed. With the coming of evening and its accompanying dampness, Kathy's bronchial condition was liable to flare, and the steady honk-honk-honk of her breath intake frightened us. We especially dreaded the winters, with their inevitable viruses.

The most famous Mongoloid child to be born during Kathy's span of life was little Robin, the daughter of Roy Rogers and Dale Evans. After Robin's death, her mother wrote the beautiful story, *Angel Unaware*. Several of our friends who had read the story urged me to read it.

When I read the tender account of Robin, I felt a kindred spirit with those parents, who had found the joy that could be theirs in loving one of these little "angels." The final chapter tells of Robin's death as a result of mumps.

On the very day I read the story, Christine was sent home from school. Her jaw was swollen and giving her some pain. *Oh, no!* I thought, and down, down, down I sank in needless despair. But it was only swollen glands!

Figuratively, we sat on a bomb most of the time. An illustration of this was an experience we had one Wednesday evening. It was my turn to stay at home with Kathy while the rest of the family attended prayer services. Our church is about a half hour's drive from our home if the traffic is heavy. I washed the supper dishes while Kathy played around the kitchen. I glanced in her direction and saw that she was having difficulty breathing.

I grabbed her and rushed upstairs to the oxygen tank. The hose was soon adjusted and I began pouring the clear air into her lungs. I managed to telephone the church, and soon the family was speeding toward Depew. I prayed as I worked, and learned later that the pastor had called on the congregation to pray for her. By the time Charlie and the girls arrived at home, she was improved. Believe me, I was the one who needed strength!

Conditions were reversed one Sunday night, for it was I who sat in our family pew. An usher whispered that Charlie had called and that Kathy wasn't well. It was my turn to speed toward home. "This is the thing I have feared," I told the girls.

When we drove into the yard, Charlie was surprised that

we had come home. The message had been misunderstood. He had just wanted to know the location of some medicine to relieve Kathy's mosquito bites.

I think our reaction at the time is typical of people who have in their home someone with a condition like Kathy's. It is easy to panic. Small things become outsized. We were too much afraid, but we couldn't seem to help it!

There were times when we feared with good reason. I recall one of them. The day had gone as usual, without any undue excitement. Charlie gave Kathy her medicine, and they carried out the usual routine of teeth-brushing. Kathy, in her pajamas, was carried upstairs by Daddy, to avoid heart strain.

I followed them and sat by her crib for a while. I listened to her prayers and read her a story. I first knew that something was wrong when I heard the low whistle at the intake of her breath. It rapidly increased until she was definitely in heart failure.

Charlie, Janice, and Chrissy raced upstairs from different rooms of the house. As we checked the oxygen tank, we discovered that the dial registered only about fifteen minutes of oxygen. We had not used it for some time, and none of us had realized that the supply was so low. The small doses we had given her at bedtime, "just for a lift," had depleted the tank!

The company which handled oxygen replacement was unable to deliver a fresh tank to us in the country, so there was nothing to do but to go after it.

Charlie began the dash by car to Buffalo for a fresh supply of oxygen. He is noted for his careful driving, but I am sure that on this occasion all caution was thrown to the winds. He must have "flown low."

The girls and I worked with Kathy. I never prayed so hard in my whole life as I did then. It was evident that Kathy was dying. Her short breaths, which were so much a part of her pattern of life, gave way to long gasps, about eight to ten per minute. I could not let her die. I prayed, with a long passionate heart cry to God, "Oh, please, don't let her die! Please, don't let her die!" I never had labored so in prayer.

Suddenly, I felt relief. I knew God had heard. She was still gasping for breath, but she was wonderful. Janice through her tears looked at Kathy and asked, "How do you feel, honey?" "Fine," Kathy answered.

We watched the dial on the tank. The hand moved relentlessly until it registered "empty," but the life-giving oxygen still poured out! We also watched the clock, and waited for the sound of the car in the driveway.

Forty-five minutes from the time this incident began, Charlie laboriously lugged the new tank up the stairs. And, with the perfect timing known only to God, the old tank sputtered and stopped at that moment! The fifteen minutes had stretched to forty-five in answer to prayer! Kathy had responded, and was soon sleeping peacefully.

I once heard a preacher say that the "perfect peace" which the Lord promised in Isaiah 26:3 is a promise for the future and is not to be appropriated now. I am inclined to agree. Either that is true, or somehow we have missed the way as far as that blessing is concerned. We did not always have perfect peace about Kathleen's condition. We did have the knowledge of the presence of the Lord, and that in itself was sufficient.

CHAPTER 9

Kathy Seems Near Normal

As TIME PASSED, we could see that Kathy was near normal. She had certain blocks in her mental development, but she was the dearest, sweetest little girl anyone could want to know.

If a child is blind, others must be eyes to the child; if a child can't hear, others must in various ways convey the message of the outside world to this child with deaf ears. Does it not follow, that if a child is not entirely whole in all areas of the mind, those who love her will help over the rough places of life?

Kathleen had definite ideas of her own. She could entertain herself, and would spend hours looking at pictures or thumbing through her storybooks. She attempted to draw, and the objects were discernible.

The neighbor children did special things for her. Dale Kivett, who lives next door, came over and played gently with her in the back yard. The Sticht children played dolls with her on our side porch.

Becky Hoffman was her friend at Sunday school. Becky is the daughter of Dr. and Mrs. Warren Hoffman, who have since moved to Ft. Wayne, Indiana.

Kathy was unusually shy, and noises bothered her greatly. If a pan was dropped, or if someone laughed loudly, she would cry with fear. She taught us to be quieter than we had been before. Even today, when someone shouts, I automatically move to shush him.

Although we in Kathy's family had no doubts concerning her mental progress, we could see that other people thought that we were only protecting her. When we told them of God's promises, they would quietly ask, "But what does the doctor say?"

We had to admit that the doctor hadn't said anything for quite a while, for he hadn't seen Kathy. Doctors had been so discouraging in the earlier days that we felt we were "on our own" and that the Lord was our Great Physician. When she became ill, we prayed, and God answered our prayers.

About this time an important event took place — our Nancy's marriage. For a couple of years, at least, it had been obvious that she would some day change her name to Morningstar. Ray and Nancy were high-school sweethearts and, after a year's engagement, the wedding date was set for June 12, 1954. Ray was heartily welcomed into our family. He is a Christian young man, athletic, and energetic. Besides this, he adored Nancy!

There was a flurry of showers and the usual excitement which attends plans for a formal wedding. Nancy was to wear her cousin Luella's gown. I was elected to make the gowns for Janice and Christine. Marilyn Olson, the maid of honor, and Edwine Hornung Swanson, Sylvia Sharpe, and David's wife Carol, the bridesmaids, were to make their own gowns.

We debated about Kathy. Did we dare to let her be the flower girl? We knew that she would carry the basket all right. We were just afraid that the excitement would damage her tricky heart. We compromised by making her the kind of dress, matching the bridesmaids' dresses, that she would have worn had she actually walked down the aisle. Ray's cousin Deann walked in her place.

Paul Dittmar, Ray's cousin, was the best man. Ushers included David, Russell Bishop, Harold Deutschlander, Jack and Paul Scheuer. C. David Schultz, Jr. served as ring bearer.

It was a beautiful day. Nancy's cousin, the Rev. Loren Moore, had come from Indiana to perform the ceremony. Loren and Phyllis and their children, Elaine and Mark, were our house guests. I wore a navy dress and hat, with touches of white, and Mrs. Morningstar wore a black print dress, with a black straw hat, and gloves. Two hundred fifty guests were present, and the reception was held in the church social hall.

Kathy behaved beautifully. She loved to look at Nancy, for she had long admired brides. The long white gown and veil fascinated her.

Charlie, who is not noted for being sentimental, leaned over to Nancy just before they started down the aisle together, and said, "I'll give you a little kiss before you go." It was so unexpected, and it touched her so deeply, that she wept all of the way to the altar.

When the reception was over, we hurried home with Kathy just in time to escape the fury of a sudden and violent thunder storm. We found that the day had taken its toll on our little girl, and it was a night of unrest as we kept the oxygen tank going.

Ray and Nancy left that evening for their honeymoon in Washington, D. C. and New York. As Nancy started toward the door, she turned and threw her arms around my neck and said, "My wedding was all I ever had dreamed of. Mom."

CHAPTER 10

Doctors are Amazed

K ATHY WAS FOUR YEARS OLD. Two years had passed since she lay "dying" in the hospital. We had developed a mania for photography. We wanted to record every move she made. We took movies and snapshots of her, trying to capture her moods for future viewing when we would want to remember.

Doctors had explained to us the pattern that the Mongoloid child follows. They had said that the growth of a normal child follows a steady line. This was illustrated on a chart showing the side of a hill. "Here is the normal child," they had said. "He progresses continually, always in an upward and forward direction. As for the Mongoloid child, he remains dormant for long periods of time, then has a sudden spurt directly vertical in his growth. He stagnates again on a level plain for a long time. Each development period is far below the climb of the normal child."

Kathy did not follow this pattern. There never was a time in her whole life when we felt that she did not show progress. We have to admit that her development was not on a par with the steady advancement of the normal child, but it was fast enough to keep us from any alarm as to her capabilities.

Christine was of tremendous help with Kathy. Kathy was "Miss Tag-a-long" and shadowed Chrissy from one place to another. Although Christine was not aware of it, she helped me a great deal by her attitude toward her younger sister. "Oh, Kath," she would say so matter-of-factly, "you can do that just as well as I can."

There was not the least hesitation in either Janice or Chrissy to take Kathy with them when they went any place. I am sure the thought did not enter their minds to be ashamed of their sister. They thought she was cute.

One night when Charlie was reading in our room and listening at the same time to Kathy's quick panting, he looked up from his book and said, "I have been thinking that maybe we had better take Kathleen to Dr. W. for a checkup to see how she is doing."

I agreed that it might be time for a change in the heart medicine. Besides, I was rather anxious to see what the doctor thought of Kathy's progress. When we told Kathy about it the next day, she wanted to go. This was an adventure to her. She enjoyed the excitement of having Mommy dress her and brush her hair, telling her meanwhile how beautiful she was. (She thought so too, as she preened before the mirror.)

Kathy loved the ride in the car, perched on my lap so that she could see out of the window. Charlie drove us in, and after he had parked the car, his big hand closed over Kathy's while she hung onto mine with her free hand. I must confess that I walked with a question in my heart. I had had the experience of hearing doctors give discouraging reports so often that I had very little hope for an optimistic one this time. So far, the medical men had pointed to signs which I, as a lay person, was not aware of.

We entered the medical building and found an elevator waiting. Kathy wasn't too happy about the sudden ascent. She obviously had forgotten the elevators at C—— Hospital. We hurried down the hall, and as we neared the doctor's office Kathy saw the dolls and toys which were inside his open door. She ran ahead of us straight to one of the dolls and, completely uninhibited, took it in her arms.

I have wished since that we could have photographed the expression on Dr. W.'s face when he saw our little girl. "Why, hello, Kathy, how are you?" he asked.

"Oh, I'm fine," she replied, too busy with his toys to bother much with him!

The doctor turned to us and remarked, "This is almost unbelievable!"

The examination went well. It included every area of her body.

Because I want you to understand our joy as we read the doctor's report of the examination later given to us, I include a portion of the report:

KATHLEEN SCHULTZ — 9/8/55
4 years and 4 months — 36¾ lbs, 38½″ tall

GENERAL APPEARANCE: Walks well and normally. Is active, eager, and not quiet for one moment, shows initiative and investigation and appears to use both of these whenever left alone.

HEAD: Well formed. The head apparently is somewhat brachycephalic but not markedly so and certainly appears normal with hair. The hair is very light, almost albinoid in color and is minimally coarse posterially but nothing spectacular. (The family says that the hair posterially was quite coarse earlier in life.)

EARS: Somewhat low set. The right one tends to slant backward and is somewhat square. They are unequal in that the left is better set and better shaped.

FOREHEAD: Appears normal, and the brow is not marked although there is some fullness in the midline.

EYES: Definitely somewhat slanted and narrow with large epicanthal folds, especially on the right, and the eye lids are also somewhat red and granular and the child blinks and squints as if there is photophobia (the family deny this and say this is a trick to get attention).

NOSE: The bridge is somewhat depressed, and nose is rounded with the tip back so that the nares look out in a typical fashion.

MOUTH: Normal, somewhat small. The jaw is narrow. The teeth are well formed but on a rather narrow plane and the palate is high-arched and quite narrow.

NECK: Not abnormal, but is somewhat full and the fat pad which was present earlier in life has completely disappeared.

CHEST: Definitely bulging anteriorly. The entire mid-portion of the chest, especially to the left, protrudes in a cup fashion over the entire precordium, is bulging forward. This does not heave as it did when originally seen. However, a palpable thrill is obvious over the entire precordium, especially the left precordium, and just under the nipple line a triple palpable beat is felt. There is a minimal Harrison's Groove, possibly only secondary to the bulge above. There is no beating of the ribs, and the chest is otherwise normal.

HEART: Percusses well beyond the nipple line and there is dullness over roughly two thirds of the anterior chest wall. The murmurs are Grade III to Grade IV at this time and are most complex. There is a prolonged systolic heard through entire systole which tends to drown out other sounds but in the background there is a to and fro murmur, as if they were both diastolic, and a systolic or presystolic heard underneath the rumbling systolic, which is most prominent at the apex. The double-type murmur is best heard at the base of the heart around the second interspace and extends fairly far out. Murmurs could be heard in the axilla and the back.

ABDOMEN: Somewhat protuberant but no liver or spleen was palpable. The liver cannot be percussed as down and the liver at this time does *NOT* appear to be enlarged. There is minimal umbilical hernia, if any, although the umbilicus protrudes.

GENITALIA: Appear normal for a girl of this age and do no longer appear puffy.

EXTREMITIES: Somewhat short and are of fairly good proportions. The hands are short and spade-like. The little finger does not reach to the distal interphalangeal joint of the fourth finger. It is short and somewhat incurved. However, the second interphalangeal bone is present as are all the interphalangeal marks. On her right hand she does not have a simian fold, on her left hand she does have a simian fold. On both hands the thumb and little finger may be extended beyond 180 degree but the hyperextension backwards of the fingers is no longer present. She is no longer hypotonic in other joints and shows no hypotonia other than the extension of the thumb and little finger.

BACK ON THE EYES: The eyes show typical Brushfield spots. These are scattered over the iris without relationship to the pattern and are at unequal distances from the pupil. They are irregular in size, shape and distribution.

IMPRESSION: Mongoloid child with a undiagnosed cardiac condition. At this time there is no evidence of failure, and the child seems to be in good condition. She has lost the hypotonicity of the Mongoloid and seems quite bright, active, and eager.

WATCH CAREFULLY. Prognosis guarded.

Doing excellent. Very active.

Live in Depew. No school for cardiacs. Try kindergarten one year late.

Accompanying the report of the examination, which was sent to the office of Dr. C, our family physician, was a letter from Dr. W. In it he reported the results of the examination and added: "However, I believe that everyone at the hospital, including myself, felt that this girl had almost no chance and if she did survive this attack, it would only be a short time before a second infection would carry her off. (He was referring to her illness at twenty-two months.) Apparently the mother's prayers were considerably more effective than our medications usually are. I am certainly happy for them with the unexpected results. Looking at her now and reading my present report, you can see how mistaken we all were. First of all, she is still alive, and second, although she is a definite Mongoloid, she seems remarkably bright and minimally hypotonic for a Mongol. Since she is doing so well, I did not change her medication."

When Dr. W. gave us this excellent report verbally, I felt that the time had come to explain to him why I had been so sure in C—— Hospital, two years before, that Kathy would progress. I told him about the revelation which I had received from the Bible on the day of her birth. He listened most attentively and respectfully and nodded his head, saying, "Yes, that is very nice."

We left the doctor's office and stepped out into the sunshine. I thought, "There never has been a day so beautiful!" My heart was thumping with such excitement and joy that it almost took my breath away. "Who can I telephone first?" I wondered, as we rode along, for, believe me, this was one piece of news I had no intention of keeping to myself!

At last, I had an answer to give to the people who asked, "What does the doctor say?" Now I could say, "He says Kathy is almost a miracle child. He says she can go to school. He says she is doing fine!"

Only the parents of children like Kathy can fully appreciate what those words meant to us. And let not Christians harshly say, "After all, wasn't God's promise enough for you?"

My only reply is this, "You just haven't been there. You haven't known what it is like to be told that your child has no mind, that your child will be grotesque. And then, to try to step out in absolute contradiction to what the experts in that field have said, and, with only naked faith, stand!" Faith had been enough for us. But can we be blamed, if we rejoiced when it was confirmed by those same men?

When we arrived at home, I walked into the dining room and opened the china closet. There, on the top shelf, was the green china cup, my token of God's promise. "I don't really need you," I said, "but I am more than glad that you reminded me often of God's covenant."

CHAPTER 11

Kindergarten at Home

In the fall of 1956, when school opened, Charlie and I tried to avoid the subject. Had Kathy been a healthy child, I would have been making her wardrobe for kindergarten. As it was, she had to remain at home, at least for another year. Her huge heart was thumping away at a terrific speed and she tired easily. Not that she said so! But, often she would lie down on the rug in the living room, just to be quiet for a while.

Kathy needed to be kept busy or she was bored. I decided that if she couldn't go to kindergarten, then kindergarten must come to her. A friend and coworker of Charlie's, Mr. Fred Boehmke, called one night to say that he had found a school desk that would be just right for Kathy. He cleaned and varnished it and, one Sunday when we returned home from church, there it was on the porch!

We turned our living room into a school with one pupil. I have no teacher's certificate, but I have taught in Sunday school and in religious instruction classes for years. I determined to teach Kathy systematically, so we obtained as many materials as possible to correspond with the public school's equipment.

We kept regular hours. Promptly at nine o'clock we had the pledge of allegiance to the flag. Then, we sang the "Star Spangled Banner." Kathy's "indivisible" in the pledge didn't come out right, but her heart was right in the matter! She enjoyed the whole procedure and especially all of the attention. That was one classroom where one pupil was definitely the favorite!

Kathy learned many things that year. I discovered later that I had expected too much of her. I had pushed her into work above her age level. I was overanxious for her to learn. I taught her the alphabet, both to write it and to recognize it. She learned numbers and what they meant. She was observant enough to match "look alike" pictures. And she kept within the lines when she colored pictures.

The girls took great interest in Kathy's progress. Every afternoon when they came home from school they sat down with her while she showed them her drawings or her printing. That was the highlight of the day for Kathy. She greeted each one with a bear hug and shouted at the top of her lungs, "Chrissy is home! Chrissy is home!" or, "Daddy is home! Daddy is home!" The neighbors said they could keep track of our activities because of our loud little announcer.

The friends who visited Janice and Christine were very kind to little Kathy. Donna Singer would shake her head and say, "That child is a miracle!" Hannah Jean Galloway was Chrissy's best friend. Hannah's dad, Fritz Galloway, and Charlie had worked together in their early years. After Fritz married, he and his wife, Ruth, became members of Prospect Church. It was natural that our families would be friendly.

Christine and Hannah Jean were born three weeks apart, Ruth and I having had a double shower preceding their arrival. As the girls grew older, they constantly visited back and forth. Kathy was the typical little sister, always getting in their hair. The girls would start for a walk, and little Miss Busybody would start after them. Each of them grabbed one of her hands and brought her back, with Kathy protesting every step of the way.

Of particular annoyance to Hannah, would be the times when Kathy raided her overnight bag. There would be a string of panties, slips, assorted pins, blouses, house slippers, and hankies over the dining room and living room floors. Hannah, in great embarrassment, would recover her belongings, threatening Kathy with punishment. The threats were ineffective because Hannah couldn't hold back the laughter when she saw how cute Kathy was about it all.

In our one-pupil kindergarten Kathleen learned to print her name, and wherever we looked, on the girls' school books, or the sheet music, or (if we weren't watchful) on the walls, there we saw KATHY SCHULTZ in bold letters. We couldn't scold. We were so happy to see it.

By this time, Kathy's vocabulary had improved considerably. "Shashy" was now "Jan" or "Janny." "Kiki" was "Christine," or at least "Kistine." She was quite intelligible, and one day I listed the number of words which she used. I could remember at least five hundred, and we felt that she was doing very well.

We battled periodically with the bronchial trouble. We lost count of the number of vaporizers that "conked out" on us. It was no wonder, for they were kept going on an eight-hour basis most of the time.

Kathy was growing taller. Her daddy said she had "the kind of legs the boys whistle at" and he would whistle to prove it! She would say, "Aw, Daddy," but she was pleased.

It was easy to see that a little girl lived at our house. There was the record player with its endless playing. It often competed with the television. There was a small organ in one corner of the room. It worked electrically, and Kathy could play the scale on it. Dolls were all over the place. Golden Books were stacked both upstairs and down. The desk was placed in the center of the living room, handy to the TV and wonderful for coloring pictures. Kathy spent a lot of time there.

We had a cat which Kathy had loved from the time it was a kitten. And the cat in turn loved Kathy. She wrapped him in a blanket and put him in her doll carriage. It was surprising how docile he remained while she pushed him around and pretended that he was her "baby."

We tried to keep the kitty outside during the summer months. Kathy would quietly open the door and let him in. "Visitor! Visitor!" she would scream, and then, "Now Mickey, you have to go outside." It was a game with her and the cat stood it patiently. So did we.

Anything Kathy loved, we loved, too. I always had had an aversion to cats, but this one I not only endured but admired. I tried to see him through the eyes of a little girl who had such capacity to love.

The grounds around our home are spacious, almost like a park, with lovely fir trees, and beds of flowers planted here and there. Janice has been our gardener. Charlie and Raymond did the construction work on a stone fireplace, and there are benches and a table near it for out-of-door picnics.

On warm spring nights after supper, Charlie and I strolled out to the benches to enjoy the fresh air while the girls washed the dishes. We were never alone very long, for, peeking around the house would be a light-haired child, wanting to be a part of the family circle. Not far behind her would sneak the cat, silently, with his eyes darting here and there for an unwary bird.

Swings, teeter-totter boards, and a sandbox were provided for Kathy's out-of-door entertainment. Her nephew and niece on the hill often came down to play. They were three mischiefs! The younger children adored Kathy, for she was just enough older to be very superior!

In spite of Kathy's defective heart, she sometimes went

exploring. What anxious minutes I spent searching for her! I found her visiting the Sticht family across the road a few times. A new kitten was the attraction. Once I spotted her rounding the corner on her way to Hollice McLeod's at the end of Zurbrick Road. We were amazed that she could walk so far. More often, she visited Nancy on the hill, even though this was absolutely forbidden territory because of the steep incline.

Kathy showed surprising strength. She asked me one day to carry her doll cradle downstairs for her. I was busy and pushed the request aside. The next thing I knew, she had gotten it to the bottom of the stairs! I surrendered and carried it to the living room. And to think that Daddy carried her upstairs every night to protect her weak heart!

She was seldom punished. But, there were times. . . . You can only stand so much! Every child must obey within reason. I spanked her a few times when all reasoning failed!

I well remember one of those times. Kathy had been in the bathroom, and when she came out, she closed the door. I was in the dining room at the sewing machine and paid no attention to her. Presently there was a trickle of water flowing out from under the bathroom door. I hurried to it and discovered that the door was locked. The rascal had placed the plug in the sink, turned on the water, pulled the inside lock down, and when she closed the door, it locked! While I struggled to find the key, Kathy doubled over with laughter. By that time, the hardwood floor in the dining room was pretty well soaked. After turning off the faucet, I said, "Sick or not, I am going to spank you for that trick!" It sobered her considerably, and I kept my word. Underneath my temper, I was delighted that she had the intelligence to concoct such an idea!

Oh, yes, there was a little girl in our house. Her closet was full of the darlingest dresses. Her sisters "couldn't resist" buying things for her. Others bought for her, too.

Everyone felt that she was only borrowed, and we all wanted to enjoy every minute of her stay with us.

Our travel, as a family, was very limited when Kathy was small. However, one weekend, which we spent at Oswego, New York, is one of our very pleasant memories. We were invited by the Rev. and Mrs. John B. Kenyon to be their guests. John was the Baptist minister there.

This was a big trip for us! We packed a lunch, and at noon Charlie, the girls, Kathy, and I sat along the roadside to enjoy it. I can still see Kathy in her striped shorts and matching top, sitting on the grass, mastering the tuna fish sandwich, and feeling like such a big girl. This was a real adventure! She was "one of the bunch."

We had a wonderful visit. John had alerted the nearest fire station that a heart patient would be visiting in his home and, although we had left the tank of oxygen at home, we felt rather secure.

We attended the Ontario Bible Conference during the weekend. Dr. and Mrs. George Alden Cole were there. Dr. Cole had been our pastor at Prospect for seventeen years, and we loved them dearly.

On Monday, Bessie Kenyon invited them to eat with us. She cooked a delicious fried chicken dinner, as only an Alabama girl can. After dinner we had a time of prayer before the good-byes were said. Douglas and David Kenyon stood with their parents to wave to us as we pulled out of the yard. Kathy had been remarkably well while we were there, and she enjoyed the vacation as much as any of us.

CHAPTER 12

Kindergarten at School

"TRY KINDERGARTEN one year late," Dr. W.'s report had said, and it was now time to "try" it. We had talked with the principal of an elementary school in Depew about entering Kathy there, and it was agreed that I would work closely with the teacher. Mrs. Sherman Hetherly had taught for twenty-five years in that school, and she advised us to request Mrs. Lynch as Kathy's teacher. "She is gentle and soft-spoken," Mrs. Hetherly had said. "I know Kathy will love her."

Kathy did love her. She enjoyed the children, too. This was far better than going to school by herself. Most little girls have a "best friend," and Kathy soon selected Mona as hers. Kathy wanted to sit next to Mona. She loved to touch Mona's hair. I think before the year was through, Mona became a little weary of the adoration. She was kind to Kathy, but didn't want to be smothered!

The other kindergarten youngsters treated Kathy like a "little sister." They helped her. I dressed her especially well, and it was a matter of interest to the children to see what Kathy was wearing each day. Some of them became friendly with me, too, for I spent so much time in school.

Not long after school started, one of the little boys had a birthday party at his home and Kathy was invited. This was very thrilling to us. We would have moved heaven and earth to get her there. The party was held in his garage, and all of the children had a good time racing around. Kathy entered into the spirit of it as much as her strength would permit. This was progress!

We were happy to see Kathy enter into the school life. She took her turn with other youngsters in taking notes to the cafeteria. She took advantage of the school equipment and used the play irons, etc. as much as the others did. She liked the big blocks and the small ones, but she sometimes held her ears when the boys were too noisy with their construction work.

Mrs. Lynch found that Kathy responded least to a direct command. This was not because she was rebellious, but because she did not fully comprehend what was expected of her. Kathy was particularly gifted in music and could keep rhythm perfectly. She entered willingly into the musical games and loved the fairy tales which were played on records. We kept her at home on Wednesdays so she could rest. This would have retarded her even if there had been no other difficulty. But she was very aware of her surroundings, as the following story proves.

Kathy and her daddy were pals. She was quick to come to his defense if she thought I was giving him a hard time. I remember one week when we had been feuding. Nothing serious. Just sniping at each other trying to "get the last word."

Charlie had a notion that I was expecting him to run too many errands. "You never say to me, 'Are you tired? Why don't you lie down for awhile?'" he complained. I filed that one away for future reference!

The next evening after supper Charlie was dozing in his lounging chair. I saw a golden opportunity to "get even," so I shook him until he was fully awake. Then I asked the pointed question, "Why don't you lie down and sleep for awhile?"

Kathy was watching our little hassle, and she knew it was partly in fun, but it worried her. Children have a way of magnifying little family differences. An incident happened the next morning that was just too much for her patience.

Charlie was hurriedly eating his breakfast. He was due at work in half an hour. As he drank his coffee, he glanced at the morning paper. Kathy was leisurely enjoying her cereal, for this was Wednesday, and she could stay at home.

Not one to let a feud die without a good solid victory, I looked at Charlie over the top of his paper and sweetly suggested, "Why don't you lie down for a while? You look tired!" That did it!

"You think you're cute!" was the most he could manage at the moment.

Kathy, taking in the situation, reached over and patted her beloved daddy on the arm. "Don't quarrel, Daddy," she soothed, and as she saw my laughter, she added, "And don't you quarrel with my daddy, either, Mommy!" She was our peacemaker.

We sometimes gently teased her just to see her eyes light with fire as she "got up her Irish." When we annoyed her too much, she gave us a scathing look and sneered, "Don't be obnoxious!" This large word, used correctly by our "Mongoloid," was delightful to us. We exulted every time she said it.

Kathy had one month-long interruption to her school year. A year or so previous to this time, Mr. John R. Peachey, president of the Loblaw Company of Buffalo and a member of Prospect Church, had been chairman of the Heart Fund drive. He had been interested in Kathy's progress since her birth, and he suggested to us one day that we consult Dr. L. at C——— Hospital to see if anything could be done for her. Dr. L. is well known in the city as a leading heart specialist for children. We took Mr. Peachey's advice and made an appointment.

As a result of the consultation, Dr. L. advised us to give our permission to an exploratory operation to determine the extent of heart damage Kathy had. We were afraid to subject her to any kind of ordeal and demurred. However, after several months, we saw that she never would be better just with medication. We agreed to the plan, and set the date for November 19, 1957.

We were afraid. How we prayed that the Lord would not take our little one from us! We tried to prepare her for the operation. She was not fearful at all and went with us very happily.

When we entered the hospital, we were assigned to a southwest room in which there was a crib, with a couch for me. As I settled down for the night I was troubled. Nancy expected her third child at any moment. And Kathy was facing diagnostic surgery.

When Charlie returned to the hospital the next morning, he told me that Nancy had been taken to the hospital. Ten minutes later, the nurse took Kathy to the operating room.

There was a gale-force wind that November day. It howled and whistled and shoved at the southern-exposed windows. Charlie sat in one chair and I in the other. We didn't talk much. We just waited. And waited. And waited.

At about 2:30 P.M. Dr. L. entered the room, carrying a weepy Kathleen. She reached out her arms to me and cried some more. It had been awful, she was trying to tell me. I tucked her into her crib, and she soon fell asleep, while her daddy held her hand.

At 4:30 Nancy's baby, Donna Ruth Morningstar, was born, and we were told all was well. The same afternoon we were informed that we would have Kathy's report the next day. Charlie stayed with her while I went down to the cafeteria for supper. On the elevator were two interns who had assisted in Kathy's operation. They were not aware of my identity, and they discussed Kathy's heart. I knew by their conversation that they thought hers was a hopeless case.

Dr. L. confirmed my suspicions the next afternoon. He described Kathy's heart damage as "very serious." "She has a large hole in the lower wall of her heart," he told us, "and we have no machine at the present time that will take over the circulation while such an injury is repaired." He continued, "I am sorry. I wish I could give you better news, but I cannot. We hope sometime to be able to cope with these things, but we can't now."

After he left, I glanced compassionately at Charlie. "It is more of the same, isn't it? I guess we shouldn't get our hopes up," I said. But how can one keep from hoping?

It was still storming when we took Kathy home. The rain splashed at the windshield as the wipers moved together in a clasped-hand effect, only to release themselves and swoop away again. Kathy was bundled in her woolen snowsuit, and I held onto her tightly as we rode along. At every traffic light, as we waited for the green signal, her daddy would lean over and reassure her that everything was fine. We would be home soon.

The ordeal had been almost too much for her. We tucked her into her own little bed and were thankful that she was safe at home again. We gave her a "booster shot" of oxygen, and she snuggled down into her pillow, soon falling asleep.

"We tried," Charlie said softly, almost apologetically. "We wouldn't have felt right to let her go without knowing for sure whether she could be helped."

There was an air of gloom around the house .The girls were conditioned to bad news by this time, but this latest news had its effect nevertheless. We wanted so much to keep her, yet we knew that we lived dangerously at all times.

Kathy had received several cards from our friends and a large box of special ones that the kindergarten children had made. Dr. William H. Lee Spratt had come to Prospect Church as pastor, and he had brought a single rose to the hospital for her. It was so fragile and beautiful, just like our Kathy. He had spent time with us, praying for us and for her. The telephone calls and cards continued to come after we were at home again. It was pleasant to go to the mailbox and find remembrances from so many well-wishers.

The next morning after we returned home, I scooted out to the mailbox and found the usual magazines, several cards and letters and an envelope from *Reader's Digest*. This was nothing new, for I had been an agent for subscriptions to that magazine for some time. Since I worked for them, they wrote to me frequently, sending the latest price lists, etc., I left that one to open last.

Finally, very casually, I opened the *Digest* letter. To my utter amazement it contained a check for a hundred dollars! I looked at Charlie across the living room and, trying to keep my voice as even as possible, said, "Oh, the *Reader's Digest* has sent me a hundred dollars."

He knows what a jokester I am, so it didn't faze him at all. He replied, "Yeah! Yeah! That'll be the day!"

Then, I took the precious piece of paper and danced over to him with it, waving it under his nose. He glanced at it, then took a good hard look. "Wowee!" he hollered.

There was a note of explanation accompanying the check. It stated that a brief story that I had submitted about three months before had been accepted for the "Laughter is Good Medicine" department. I had sent many such stories, and had come to the conclusion that it was impossible to make the grade. Here was living proof that anyone could do it. Especially if they had an ingenious husband who would put good whiskey into his radiator for anti-freeze, because he was an "abstaining Baptist" and didn't know what else to do with the Christmas gift.

The money could not have come at a more opportune

time. Besides, we needed a little good news for a change. The check proved to be a diversion for us. We spent the rest of the day good-naturedly arguing about who it rightfully belonged to. Charlie said that he would have to claim it, for he was the subject of the story. I countered that if I hadn't written the story, there would have been no check. We compromised by spending it for medical bills, as we had known all the time.

Although the story had been written with my name withheld, we received notes from Florida and Nebraska from people who knew us and "just knew that the policeman was Charlie." We also had a telephone call from dear friends at Salisbury, Maryland who were amused by the article and who had heard the story before it appeared in print.

Kathy's strength returned sooner than we expected. In only a few weeks she was in school again. She was the "heroine" as the children crowded around her to hear all about the hospital. She acted very matter-of-course and shrugged them aside.

It was a very busy year for me. We took Charlie to the bus stop on our way to school, and then I took Kathy to her room. If it was one of her stubborn or difficult days, I had to stay an hour or two. When she was settled, I would hurry home to do housework, and rush back to school again in the afternoon.

I held a part-time job at the time. In 1954 Mr. Richard Bennett, owner and editor of the *Depew Herald* and *Lancaster Enterprise* had offered me a job as reporter. He had also agreed to print a poetry column entitled: "Thoughts Along the Way" which would contain an original weekly poem. Later, the work was expanded to include feature stories.

All in all, there was never a dull moment. All of my work was done at home by telephone. On the days when I collected news, Kathy sat at her desk with a telephone (which

Dad had gotten for her). With pencil in hand, she pretended to collect news, too. If there was school that day, she took her place at the desk as soon as she got home.

At the end of the school year, Kathy received her report card. It read as follows: 53 school days absent. Knows address. Can count to 20. Is able to read numbers. Is able to write numbers. Improving in the understanding of the meaning of numbers and their terms. Follows lines from left to right. Improving in telling stories from pictures and recognizing rhyming words. Learns rhymes and poems. Takes part in dramatic play. Is improving in speech and in listening while others are speaking. Sings simple songs. Responds to rhythm activities. Enjoys listening to music. Improving in pasting and drawing simple forms. Rests quietly. Uses handkerchief. Plays and works safely. Works quietly. Takes care of materials. Improving in working and playing well with others, finishing work, and cleaning after work. (I could understand perfectly why she wasn't good at cleaning up after her work. She had too many older ones at home to baby her!)

The most important item on the report card said simply, "Assigned to Grade I, beginning September, 1958." O happy day! Another plateau reached!

CHAPTER 13

Happiness at Court St. School

Mrs. Loraine McCarthy, principal of Kathy's school, strongly advised us not to enter Kathy in the regular first-grade class in September. She pointed out because of the keen competition Kathleen would be unhappy. No one has time to help the one who lags too far behind. She said that a class is taken at a rather rapid pace up the ladder of learning, and it would be a frustrating experience to our little girl. "She is happy, now," Mrs. McCarthy said, "but she won't be if she is pushed too hard." We respected her advice.

On the first day of school, we took Kathy to the ungraded class in the school. As we walked along, we saw the children who had been Kathy's friends the year before. They called out to her as she passed, and she responded brightly. Then she saw Mona. Immediately she ran to get in line with the other children, because she knew that she belonged in the same class with Mona. I could see how this affected Charlie. My own heart began to pound as I felt the weight of this separation of our little one from the others. I wasn't sure how much of it Kathy understood.

I took her hand and gently pulled her away from the other children and on down the hall. We entered a rather dismal room with some desks in it. There weren't enough seats to go around. There was none to fit Kathy's short legs. She had to sit on the floor.

There were two fourteen-year-old retarded boys in the room, as well as nine younger boys who were three or four years older than Kathy. One lone girl, about twelve years old, sat at a desk reading.

The teacher flitted around in a rather abstract fashion, doing the best she could with her charges. She told us confidentially that there was one boy whom she "couldn't seem to bring out," so she herded them all, including Kathy, down to the gym, where they played roughhouse ball and jumped rope.

There was our Kathy on the gym floor, bewildered, trying to keep out of the way of the older children. I confess that it was *my* heart that was failing that morning as I saw our fragile daughter in that situation.

The teacher did not want us to stay through the morning. She walked to the front door of the school with us. As we walked, I wondered how the older kids were treating Kathy.

The tears began to stream down my face even before I was out of the building. By the time I arrived at home, I was almost in a state of collapse. "I can't do it," I kept telling Charlie. "I can't leave her there every day! Surely the Lord is not going to ask this of me. I shall keep her at home, rather than this!" I sobbed.

Charlie tried to comfort me, but he was as disturbed as I. He turned on the radio to "Good News at Noon," which is broadcast by our friend, the Rev. Alan T. Forbes, director of the Youthtime Center in Buffalo. His devotional program is on the air every noon hour, and I am a daily listener.

On this particular day Alan had chosen to read a poem of mine from my first published book, *Thoughts Along the Way*. Before reading the poem, he said some very kind things about me. It was balm to my pained soul. He could not have timed it more perfectly.

I managed to regain my composure. Since we had some

immediate problems to settle concerning Kathy's schooling, this was no time for hysterics. We could still place her in the regular first-grade class, but we did not want to impose a hardship on her in any way. Then we thought of Charlie's sister Anna.

Anna, whose husband had died, was working as secretary at the Court Street School in Lancaster. Anna had been more than a relative; she had also been our friend through the years. She had told us about the three classes for the "different" children in Lancaster, the primary special, the intermediate special and the junior high special classes. Carefully trained teachers are hired for these classes for the exceptional children.

"If only we could place Kathy at Court Street School," Charlie said. He called his sister to see if there was any possibility of doing so. She conferred with Principal Donald Perrine, who understood our situation and cooperated with us immediately. We told him how well Kathy had gotten along in kindergarten at the school she had been attending but that the special class there did not fill her requirements. He replied, "Bring her tomorrow."

Miss Lillian Pettit was Kathy's teacher. The room was geared to the needs of seven-, eight- and nine-year-olds. There was a toilet, with a sink, just the right size for little folks. The tables and chairs were comfortable, and there were so many things to play with and to learn from. One wall was entirely of windows, and when the sun streamed in, it made everybody happy. How we loved that room! And how we appreciated the efforts on the part of everyone to develop these handicapped children to the zenith of their possibilities.

We also were assured that after three years in the primary class, Kathy could be promoted to the intermediate group, where she would continue to receive specialized teaching.

What a lot of fun they had! They went to the A & P

Store and learned how to shop. They made cookies right in school. They had tea parties for their mothers and — sometimes — fathers. They decorated their own Christmas trees. They walked to the library (a feat which almost finished Kathleen, for the teacher had forgotten about the heart condition until they were almost to their destination). However, after a day's rest at home, she was all set for another excursion.

I believe that the most important feature sponsored by the ungraded classes is the presenting of an assembly program. At least, it was an important occasion for our family.

The big day was approaching for Miss Pettit's special class. The children were jumping around more than usual and shouting back and forth. They were plying the teacher with endless questions and tattling on each other constantly. "Jimmy isn't standing on the tape." "Allen is unrolling the flag." "Gerry is hiding behind the curtain." The primary class was going to be in the spotlight at the assembly program. Teacher and pupils were nervous.

Several months before, our seven-year-old towhead had acquired a record of "Snow White and the Seven Dwarfs." After hearing it at least a hundred times, I knew that this was it! If anything would push me over the brink into the paper-doll-cutting island, that record would! "Snow White, Snow White, loveliest maiden of all," I heard repeatedly.

It wasn't that I had anything against Snow White, the poor dear! It was just that I felt we had sympathized with her enough. Maybe the rest of us hadn't been lost in the woods, but we all had our troubles! And they were not settled by the discovery of a beautiful little cottage with rent and board free!

Kathy had a vivid imagination and pantomimed the record with adeptness. The pathos she threw into the poisoned apple scene was something to behold! She tossed herself onto the floor with such violence that if the apple had actually been in her mouth, it would have dislodged immediately, I am sure.

It was a natural that "Snow White" would form the basis for the assembly program. The special class was not exactly bursting with talent, and even the coordinating of the twelve youngsters into a common project was a man-sized job. But youthful Miss Pettit was willing to tackle it. Therefore when Miss Pettit learned that one child had already practiced such a dramatic production, she grabbed at the stroke of luck.

I went to the final rehearsal before D day. (That stands for Dread day for the poor teacher.) Allen carried the flag to the platform, and Gerald Clark was the announcer. With much shouting and scolding from the teacher, the children whipped through the rehearsal with only minor incidents, such as Kathy pushing too hard on the cardboard house, and felling the whole side of it to the floor, resulting in a gush of tears.

On the big day I decided to keep Kathy at home until almost time for the program to begin. I bathed her and began to get her ready. I set up the ironing board and turned on the iron. (I had washed a yellow dress for her to wear, dried and sprinkled it, and it was ready to iron. It was a darling embroidered cotton that had been the handiwork of my niece, Phyllis Moore.) To save time, I dashed upstairs to change my own dress and comb my hair. I suddenly had an uneasy feeling. Kathy never had touched the iron, but there could be a first time. I hurried downstairs. My hunch was right! The iron was placed directly on the folded dress and the cloth was smoldering. I gave a sad low cry and snatched the iron away. The dress was ruined!

I knew that Kathy had not done this to be naughty. She was trying to help. I didn't have the heart to scold her. I just went upstairs and cried. What could I do now? What in the world would she wear for this important day in her life? Nancy came to the rescue with another yellow dress which she had been saving for her little Janice.

I never shall forget the production "Snow White" as interpreted by Miss Pettit's class. The auditorium was well filled with the first three grades of the school and their teachers. There was a spirit of anticipation among the little folks. The lights were dimmed, and the program began. Kathy and I sat near the front so that she could make her appearance at the proper time. I could see that the ancient foe of actors, stage fright, was making inroads into her calmness.

Gerry stood in the spotlight, said in his best voice, "We will now present Snow White and the Seven Warts." There wasn't a snicker! It was plain to see that the children had been threatened ahead of time as to their behavior. This was one afternoon when they weren't to laugh, no matter what happened!

The record had been retaped to include inserts of the other material. As the tape began to play, the children took their places for the pantomime. As the story unfolded, it was time for the appearance of Snow White. Snow White rebelled! I coaxed and pleaded, but she sat and shook.

I finally persuaded her to sit on the little stool at the front of the platform. Then, as the voice told of the woodsman who took Snow White into the forest to be killed, Gerry, the nine-year-old Negro boy, grabbed Kathy unceremoniously, and away they went to the pseudo forest.

This action loosed the tears which had been hovering in Kathy's eyes. As the song rang out clearly, "Poor Snow White, lost in the woods," Kathy stood crying in the wilderness. It fit in perfectly — so much so that everyone's heart went out to her. This was more than acting! These tears were for real!

After the first emotion had subsided, Kathy got into the swing of things and grabbed the broom to sweep out the little cottage for the seven dwarfs. She danced around with the others, in just the proper mood. When the final scene was enacted, everyone mourned the little blond princess who lay on the stage awaiting the kind prince, who would take her away from it all.

It was a great day! Kathy received many compliments for her part in the school program. Again we remembered to thank the Lord for another plateau, another ledge achieved on the mountain of faith.

At the beginning of the school year, Dr. Allen Kuntz, school psychologist, had put Kathleen through a series of tests to determine her IQ and to learn her capabilities.

We went to his office for a conference, having conditioned ourselves for a discouraging report. However, he was very encouraging. He showed us in detail what his tests had consisted of, and he also explained how she had responded. He also said, "Now, I make no pretense of being a medical man, but I don't think Kathy is Mongoloid at all."

We assured him that all the medical doctors who had seen Kathy were agreed that she was a Mongoloid. Then he continued, "Kathy has good possibilities. She can be educated. She is more intelligent than the children who can simply be trained. She can have a limited education." He showed us a chart where Kathy had drawn two characters. "Those are pretty good drawings of men, I would say," and he did.

We left Dr. Kuntz's office on "cloud nine." We asked ourselves, could it be that the tide was turning and that Kathy would have a better life than we had dared to hope?

Now, after a year at Court Street School, we could see that Dr. Kuntz' prediction had been correct. Kathy was learning. She was happy and growing. She was holding her own physically, and she was our joy.

CHAPTER 14

Illness, Followed by Happy Days

In the spring of 1959 a virus attacked Kathy's frail body. She had had minor ailments before, but this was serious. Her temperature mounted, her appetite waned, her heart faltered, and again we despaired of her life. We had thanked the Lord many times for the new antibiotics, which we had used freely. This time they were instrumental in saving her life.

She seemed even more fragile after this ordeal. The first time I bathed her in the tub, I had to turn my face away to hide the tears. Her body looked exactly like the pictures I have seen of children in Europe who suffered from malnutrition. Her knee bones were larger than her thighs. I could count every rib. Her stomach was hollowed out. We marveled that she survived at all.

Janice told us later that she could hardly get through her classes at State Teachers College because she expected to find, when she returned home, that Kathleen had passed away. Once again Kathy was spared to us. This was not the Lord's time. We were more determined than ever to make every moment count in our enjoyment of her.

One beautiful summer day, we went to Akron State Park. In spite of the sunshine, the weather was cool enough for comfort. We found a peaceful spot where a trickle of water runs along the base of the trees. The water was not deep enough for swimming, but it was deep enough for wading or for skimming pebbles across its surface.

We ate hamburgers in round soft rolls, with plenty of relish. There were fruit and cookies, milk for the children and coffee for us. Charlie and I lazed around while the children, with so much more energy, went from swing to swing, trying all of the park equipment. Kathy was the "biggest duck in the puddle," and she was in the puddle most of the time, loving the feel of the water on her feet.

There were several picnics that summer. We took the girls swimming, but we had to limit Kathy, for her enthusiasm exceeded her stamina. She was completely unafraid, which caused us to be more watchful of her.

When Charlie had a day off from work, Kathy tagged at his heels like a friendly puppy. If there were bills to pay, she went along. When he went to the bank, she sat demurely on the bench inside the door and waited for him to transact his business. When he went to Loblaw's, she rode in the cart and helped select the groceries. He had to watch her, or at the end of the shopping tour, there were more groceries than he wanted!

It was a common sight in Murphy's five-and-ten-cent store to see a very large man and a tiny blond girl walking hand in hand, looking at the various counters — Charlie and Kathy.

When he really wanted to shop, he sat her on a stool at the food counter, and bought a soda for her. Then, while she was busy with the drink, he could shop more quickly.

One day when he returned, Kathy was munching on a large hot dog. Her startled father looked at the clerk inquiringly. "She told me to give her a hot dog with the works," the clerk explained. Charlie gladly paid for the sandwich, jubilant that she had shown so much initiative.

There were times when Kathleen didn't feel well enough

to go to church on Sunday evening. Then Charlie would
stay at home with her. She wasn't content just to read
stories or look at television. She wanted to play games. One
of her favorite games was to play sheriff like the westerns.
She used a jump rope and tied her father's hands and feet.
Over and over again she would secure the rope around his
hands, and try to make it difficult for him to get free.

One night when they were engaged in this game, Charlie
became alarmed because try as he would, he couldn't
loosen the rope. He pulled and tugged, but she had done
a good job. Her eyes sparkled as she realized that her
daddy was really tied up. Charlie said later that he couldn't
remember when he had felt such panic. After about ten
minutes, he managed to loosen the knot. There was no
more of that game for a while! I said that if they were
able to play such gruesome games, they should be able to
go to church. But I had to admit that the quietness at home
was better for Kathy's poor overworked heart.

The girls tried to make life pleasant for Kathy. They
took her for a bus ride to Lancaster one day. That was a
real lark for her. Before school had closed, they had taken
her to concerts at the high school. Afterward, they took
her around and introduced her to their teachers. None in
Kathy's family was ashamed of her or apologized for her.
All who knew us were aware of the great love we had for
this little "bird with the broken wing."

Charlie thought of many pleasant surprises. One day he
offered to take us to Niagara Falls. Kathy was excited and
couldn't wait to get started. By ten o'clock we were on our
way over the throughway, then across the Peace Bridge.
Jan, Chris, and Kathy sat in the back seat of the car, and
as we rode along, with Dad at the wheel, they sang choruses
and played games to pass the time away. The girls watched
for interesting things to show Kathy.

The day included a visit to two elderly aunts of Charlie

and a stop at the Presbyterian Cemetery in Lewiston. This quiet spot behind the lovely white Presbyterian Church always had fascinated Charlie. It was there that most of his mother's family had been buried. It was there, years before, that he had read the tombstone of his grandmother Nancy Grove and had determined, if some day he had a daughter, to name her Nancy. One brother and two sisters of Charlie had died as children, and their graves also were there.

On the day of our visit Kathy ran among the stones and sniffed the flowers that had been placed on the graves. She tried to make a collection of flags (from the soldiers' graves), but fortunately we noticed what she was doing in time to replace them.

The sun was beginning to cast rather long shadows from the western sky, so we piled into the car again for the journey home. Our final stop was at a dairy where we had milk shakes.

The happiness of that outing was filed away in our memories. Later when the sad days would come, we would recall that happy day.

CHAPTER 15

Consultation About Heart Surgery

KATHY HAD COMPLETED two full years at Court Street School, and in the summer of 1959 a third year was coming up. She was growing tall, and I had to let out hems and buy bigger-sized patterns to make new dresses as we prepared her for school.

A new teacher was coming to the special primary grade in Lancaster. Her name was Judith Koffed. She was a quiet-voiced small girl, and had just graduated from Buffalo State Teachers College. She had met Janice at school and for this reason was very much interested in our Kathy.

One afternoon before school started, Judy and her fiancé Bob Smith stopped to see Kathy. They persuaded her to take a ride with them over to school. Kathy had shown signs of rebelling at going back to school, so we were trying to make it less complicated. As I watched the young couple drive away with Kathy sitting between them, I had a strange feeling, for she had never before gone away without a member of the family with her. This precaution was taken because of the nature of her heart ailment.

After an hour, Judy and Bob returned with Kathy, who was enjoying an ice cream cone. We were thankful for this personal interest shown by her new teacher and knew that when fall came, Kathy would be in good hands.

At first, when school started, I had some mental qualms

about Miss Koffed, for she was so small-voiced. I thought, *She will be yelling with the loudest of them after a few months with this crew.* I was wrong. She remained calm throughout her period of teaching. Her calmness quieted the children, and they all talked more softly. She had very good order. She was an excellent teacher. All of the special teachers were.

Kathy made friends among her classmates. Judy Kish called, and they had long telephone conversations. They actually didn't say much, but they enjoyed the contact. Chris would tell Kathy what to say, so the conversation kept going.

Another friend was Tommy Clark. He was such a sweet boy, and when I visited school, he would sit on my lap. He was perfectly normal at birth but at the age of two contracted a high fever. For days and days he hung between life and death. The outcome of the sickness was a limited mind. I was especially sorry for his fine-looking parents. They were heartbroken over the tragedy in their lives, but they loved Tommy dearly. All of the parents of children in the special classes had a common bond.

Little Jimmy Butters was the comedian in the class. We all love Jimmy. Born of Scottish parents, he has a pronounced brogue. One day in an endeavor to be friendly, Janice said, "Hello, Jimmy, what are you doing?" "What does it look like I'm adoin'?" he replied. I guess it was a silly question for anyone could see that he was playing ball!

Then, there were the others — all of them Kathy's friends: Gloria, whose black face was so sweet as she quietly obeyed the teacher's commands. Lynette Kennedy, a pretty little red-haired girl; Joel Freedman, and others. We affectionately called them "the motley crew." Each one had his own particular problem. Perhaps the reason Kathy was sent to us was to give us a tender heart for all defective children.

We could tell that the teacher was working with Kathy

to improve her speech. As we rode along in the car, Kathy would read the signs. "S-T-O-P," she would spell, and then very firmly pronounce the word. "F-I-R-E," she would say, and then overemphasize the *F*.

Others were noticing that Kathy was learning. When we visited Dr. C. one day, Kathy named all of the letters on a magazine there in his office.

The newspapers were carrying more and more stories about successful heart operations. We would clip them and show them to each other and wonder, *Dare we hope?* Friends kept us posted on cases they knew, and the results. Relatives wrote, "With the tremendous strides the medical profession is making in this area, you have every reason to expect that something can be done for Kathy."

I decided to call Dr. L. again to ascertain if there had been any new developments at C—— Hospital. He replied in the affirmative and gave an optimistic picture of the progress. He told me that Dr. T. had been added to the staff and was doing open-heart surgery at the hospital. He made an appointment for us to consult with Dr. T., and Charlie arranged to take the day off on that date.

Kathy went with us to the hospital, and we waited in a room with several other families until we were called. When we were taken into the consultation room, we saw Dr. L., Dr. T., Dr. V., and others seated at a table. Charlie and I sat across from them. Kathy climbed on my lap. They didn't pull any punches. They were almost brutally frank. They wanted us to be fully aware of the hazards of open-heart surgery. It was by no means a sure thing.

Dr. T. said the operation could do one of three things — make her heart worse, give her further brain damage, or heal her completely. He did not have to tell us that it might also take her life. We knew that. On the optimistic side, the surgeon told us that a large percentage of such operations were successful. We liked Dr. T. We admired his honesty. We also had every confidence in Dr. L.

I was more afraid of the brain damage than anything else. I told them that Kathy was doing so well, as they could see, that we wouldn't want anything to upset her progress. Then, realizing that I should tell them that our confidence was in the Lord and not in man, I said, "It has been the Lord who has brought her this far, and I don't believe He will let anything happen to her at this time." Charlie asked them many pertinent questions, which they kindly answered. His chief concern was reflected by the question, "How many survive?" I confess that we were both afraid.

We came home and prayed about it. We said, "Lord, give us wisdom. Don't let us make a mistake in this." Then we decided that the only way we could know the Lord's will was to proceed as far as He permitted and trust Him to stop us if we were going in the wrong direction.

We were surprised to learn that the heart surgery team had already been booked for many months ahead. The earliest date that we could possibly have would be in July of 1960, or even September. We agreed to call after the first of the year to confirm the date.

The hospital takes rather elaborate steps to prepare people who are involved in this kind of operation. Even before the exploratory operation, we had been called to the hospital where a staff worker took an hour to explain the procedure in detail and to answer any questions we might have. I had told her rather emphatically that we did not need this. I told her that we were already prepared, for we were Christians and the Lord was our strength and refuge. She misunderstood my statements and thought we were rather avoiding the issue. We met with her and I am sure that she intended to allay our fears. The Christian's source of comfort is the Lord. No other assurance can be completely dependable.

Soon afterward the rush of the holiday season was upon us. We are still a little pagan in our way of celebrating Christmas, for we have the urge to go out and buy anything in sight for our children. We jostle through the crowds with the strongest of them, and come home with tired feet, aching backs, and a glow of happiness.

We had an unusually good Christmas that year, healthwise. It was the first Christmas we could remember when Kathy didn't have a fever or some other ailment that confined her to the house. We had more freedom to drive around the city to see the lights. I still can hear Kathy's delighted squeals at the Christmas displays. She particularly enjoyed the Santa in the department store that sent out a merry "Ho! ho! ho!" every few minutes.

In our house the children have the fun of helping trim the Christmas tree, and that Christmas Kathy was right there hanging tinsel and handing Janice and Chrissy the ornaments to place in a higher spot than she could reach. She had helped trim the tree in Miss Koffed's room, so she was "sperienced."

At Christmas, and also at Easter, the Depew Police Reserves sought out children who were chronically ill and others who were in financial straits to make the holiday brighter for them. Every year, since Kathy was two years old, the Depew fire engine had clanged down Zurbrick Road, followed by cars carrying other "helpers." At Christmas time Santa came knocking at our door with candy and presents. A look under his mask revealed Walter Schneider, Depew's traditional Santa Claus. On Easter Saturday, a large bunny appeared, sometimes accompanied by other storybook characters. Kathy was gleeful over these visits.

Christmas, 1959, was no exception. Cheerful Santa came by with a beautiful doll for Kathy. How she hugged it! Her natural affection spilled over to toys and books, and especially to dolls. She examined the doll's dress and bonnet, and began arguing with Chrissy about a name. I don't know which name won.

As we celebrated the wonderful season an irritating thought kept pushing into my mind. Would this be Kathy's last Christmas with us? I was thinking of the heart surgery.

CHAPTER 16

Kathy Wants to Go to Heaven

THROUGH THE YEARS since our marriage we have tried to maintain family devotions in our home. With the diversified interests of the members of our family, it has not been easy to find a suitable time for this worship. For the most part, we have had our Bible reading and prayers immediately after breakfast. Of necessity, they were brief, but on Saturday mornings, extra time could be given.

One Saturday in January Charlie read the portion of Scripture, and Janice and Christine prayed. Then it was Kathy's turn. She folded her hands, closed her eyes and began, "Dear Lord, thank you for everything. Bless Daddy. Bless Mama. Bless Janice. Bless Chrissy. Help Christine to to be good. [This always made her sisters giggle.] Bless Carol and big Dave, little Dave, Billy, Kelly, Susan, and Timmy. Bless Ray, Nancy, little Raymond, Janice, and Donna." And then, she startled us with the following: "Lord, I would love to come to Heaven to see Jesus, and help my family to understand."

From that time on, she talked a great deal about Heaven. The cold chills played up and down my spine when she spoke in this fashion, for we knew that heart surgery was just ahead.

Kathleen was a lovely little Christian girl. Since babyhood she had gone with us to Sunday school and church.

Except when she was ill, we took her to the Sunday evening services and often to prayer meeting on Wednesdays.

Kathy listened intently when the pastor gave the message. A new minister had come to the church, the Rev. Donald A. Swartz, and Kathy loved him right away. She heard him tell of the love of God, and she knew God loved her. He said that in order to go to Heaven, it was necessary to repent of one's sins and take Jesus into the heart. Sometimes at the close of the sermon, Pastor Swartz would ask, "Is there anyone here who would like to receive the Lord Jesus Christ?" Kathy's little hand would be raised. She wanted to receive the Lord.

Pastors do not always notice the children who respond to this invitation, but that did not deter Kathy. She whispered to me, "I have to see Pastor."

"What do you want to see him about?" I asked.

"I want to tell him that I love the Lord," she said.

She became obsessed with the notion that she must make him understand that she loved the Lord. She would go to him after every service, take his hand, and give him a little curtsy in her quaint way. "Pastor, I love the Lord," she would say.

Pastor Swartz was pleasant to her and assured her, "I know you do, Kathy." But, each time the invitation was given, she was sure he gave it for her.

One day, as Kathy sat at our kitchen table watching me wash the dishes, she asked, "Mama, how can I get to Heaven?"

"Oh, I don't know," I replied. "But Jesus said He would go and prepare a place for us."

"But how can I get there?" she insisted.

"I'm not sure," I told her. "I think He sends His angels to get us when He is ready for us."

She was quiet for a while. Then she said, "What are their names?" It was all very real.

"I don't know their names," I explained, "but I am sure they will be very nice." She was satisfied.

Another day, Kathy sat with folded hands, looking out of the window. "I'm not afraid," she suddenly spoke. I looked at her rather surprised. She continued, "I'm not afraid of anything. God will take care of me."

One night I heard Kathy's voice in the dark. I hurried to her bed, and she wanted to talk. I lay down with her and she confided to me, "I am not afraid of the dark, Mama. Jesus will take care of me."

"Yes, that's right," I comforted her. "You love Jesus, don't you?"

"Yes," she assured me, "Jesus is up in Heaven to save me." I silently thanked the Lord again for letting this little one share these precious thoughts with me.

The Lord had faithfully kept His promise to make Kathy a joy. She was always cheerful. She was our peacemaker. "Don't quarrel," she would tell her sisters when they squabbled. "Don't be impatient," she would encourage her frustrated Daddy. Sometimes she would say to him, "Don't worry," with a pat on his arm.

After the first of the year, we all agreed that Kathy was getting tired of school again. Her rebellion followed a pattern. She would open one eye and squint at me. Then she would ask, "Can I stay home today?" She accentuated the positive. If I gave a negative answer, she curled into a ball and turned over as if to say, "Don't bother me. I'm too comfortable." If I assured her, "This is Saturday," she bounced out of bed, gaily thumped down stairs and snapped on the television for a wonderful morning of children's programs.

She really did seem to be a bit weary when we brought her home after the school day. Exhausted, she would lie down on the living room floor.

We tried to put a spark in the day's activity by taking

Kathy for a treat after school. She liked that part of school!
When she came running out to the car, she would ask, "Are
we going to Robert's for french fries?" Sometimes it was to
Schneider's for a pineapple sundae and a glass of water.
If the waitress forgot the water, Kathy would remind
her of it.

One day when I dressed Kathy for school, I noticed that
she had blotches of a rash on her skin. Concerned, I asked
her father to take a look at it and try to diagnose the ailment. (He was our doctor whenever there were cuts or sore
throats.) Was it measles? It couldn't be chicken pox; she
had gotten through that disease several years before. When
I put her into a tub of warm water, it had no effect on the
rash. In fact, the pinpoint marks seemed to fade more at
that time. Kathy's gums were also showing signs of bleeding.
We found that so simple a matter as brushing the teeth
caused excessive bleeding.

We decided that it would do no harm to take Kathy to
Dr. C. for an examination. It was strictly routine. Not sure
what the rash could be, he advised that we have her checked
at C——— Hospital as a precautionary measure. He suggested
a blood count too, since she was experiencing some loss of
blood.

With no thought of hurry, we waited for a week before
calling the hospital. I talked with Dr. T. and asked if a date
had been set for Kathy's operation. As an afterthought, I
mentioned the rash underneath Kathy's skin and wondered
if he should check it before surgery. He gave an affirmative
reply and, with seeming haste, made an appointment for
the next day.

Kathy was delighted to miss school. She didn't mind too
much that she was to see a doctor. Doctors had been a very
necessary part of her young life. She always questioned if
he would give her a "skeeto bite," but otherwise she enjoyed her "star" role.

We experienced the usual wait at the hospital. We watched the children and their parents come and go, although it was usually the mother who accompanied the child. Kathy was lucky that her daddy always was there, too!

We were particularly attracted to the receptionist at the desk, sad-faced but efficient. The nameplate read, "Mrs. O'Neill." She was about forty, with dark, short hair and a trim figure. When she noticed the bleeding of Kathy's gums, she seemed even more solicitous. We learned later that she had lost a three-year-old child with the same ailment the doctor would tell us Kathy had.

Since Dr. L. was out of town, Dr. V. examined Kathleen. She tried to pronouce his name, but she couldn't quite make it. She settled for "Dr. Flip Flap." He was not noticeably amused. What she lacked in an audience with him she found with her sisters later, for they latched on to the "Flip Flap" idea, and maneuvered different approaches to the subject just to hear her repeat it.

Dr. V. examined Kathy in the heart region, and gave careful attention to her glands and the inside of her mouth. "Does she bruise easily?" he wanted to know. We said she did not. He asked us to remain and meet Dr. S., a blood specialist, who would test Kathy to determine the cause of the skin condition.

The cardiac department is on the second floor of the hospital. Now, we were introduced to the third floor. We went up another flight of stairs. I was puffing and hobbling as usual, and Charlie carried Kathy to avoid any strain to her heart. At the end of the hall was a water fountain. Since Charlie was nervous and his throat was so dry, he stopped for a drink. Our practical joker couldn't let that opportunity go by, so she shoved her father's head into the water, with a good deal of splashing. It was a light moment in the midst of our concern.

Dr. S. was waiting for us. After greeting us cordially, he invited us into his office where he asked us a few questions before hoisting Kathy onto the table for another examination.

Dr. S. was a ruddy-skinned man, about forty, and six feet tall, entirely unpretentious. My observant husband mentioned the red clay on his overshoes nearby looked like mud from the Boston Hills. Surprised, the doctor said Charlie was right. He lived out Hamburg way.

A picture of a threatening storm above the table where Kathy lay was almost an omen to me. Stormy days ahead! The picture was done in oils and portrayed a field of wheat, standing in a windless field. A straight road cut a swath between fields, and resembled the roads of northern Indiana. Dark clouds rolled above the wheat. A moment of uneasiness came to this farmer's daughter, who instinctively wondered if the field could be harvested before the storm.

Dr. S. did not indicate anything unusual in Kathy's condition. He remarked about the pounding heart, her happy smile, and lovely blond hair. He dismissed us with the assurance that as soon as he had a report on the blood count, he would call us.

We joked on the way home about how Kathy had introduced us to so many doctors. Several of them were specialists. Here was another one to add to our list! As usual, Kathy worked her father for a pineapple sundae at Schneider's. He grinned sheepishly and said, "Aw, that's the least we can do!"

We had hardly gotten home when Nancy called. She was anxious to know what the doctor's report had been. I answered optimistically that there didn't seem to be anything to worry about. We were all relaxed and happy, except for the shadow of the coming operation.

In a day or two, we heard from the doctor again. This man didn't lose any time, we agreed. He said he would like to do a bone-marrow test on Kathy. This was new to us and we were not aware of what it implied. The test consists of shoving a long needle into the hip socket to withdraw some marrow. I was asked to hold Kathy down while it was being done. She screamed violently. I must have paled, for the nurse suddenly said, "Why don't you sit down?" Looking at me, the doctor insisted on my being seated.

I was thoroughly ashamed of myself, for I have tried to take things as they come without too much show of emotion. But, this was too much! I couldn't stand to see Kathy suffer. Charlie stayed though, and helped to quiet her until the ordeal was over.

"I shall call you tomorrow and let you know what the results of the test are," Dr. S. assured us. Then, as we questioned him further, "It may be one of a number of things. It may be something minor or something very serious."

I perked up at this, and asked quietly, "When you say 'something serious' what do you mean?"

His answer was one word: "Leukemia."

CHAPTER 17

Morning Up There—and Joy for Kathy

LEUKEMIA! Oh, no! Both Charlie and I sought the place of prayer. Could we ask for Kathy's healing as at other times? Somehow we both knew that we could not. This was real trouble, and we had to wait and see. There was no additional promise forthcoming.

On Thursday morning, March 10, 1960, the day after the bone-marrow test, the secretary from Dr. S.'s office called. All she said was, "The doctor would like to see you in his office at four this afternoon."

"Shall we bring Kathy with us?" I asked.

"No," she answered, "just you and your husband are to come in this time."

I placed the receiver on the phone and felt that now familiar feeling of shock. *It must be leukemia*, I thought.

When I gave Charlie the message, I did not elaborate on my fears to Charlie. I could tell by his face that he, too, was afraid.

Dr. S. came immediately to the point after we were seated in his office. "The tests show what I feared. It is acute leukemia. Scientists are working on a cure for this disease, but nothing has been discovered that permits me to hold out to you any hope for Kathy."

Her father looked at his hands for a moment before replying. "What can we do to make her comfortable?" he asked.

104

Then he added, "We will do anything!" I sat silently, trying to adjust to the confirmation of my suspicions. Then I asked, "How long will it be?"

He was the brisk doctor again. He told us there was a possibility she could last for several months. Some live even longer. He said that an older person can live with leukemia for several years, but a child usually goes more quickly.

Then he explained his method of treatment. There are three drugs he tries. He again reminded us that none of them would cure. These drugs only temporarily retard the disease. He ordered medicine for Kathy, giving us minute instructions as to its use. He warned us to protect her from bumps, particularly about the head. He made an appointment for the following week, after explaining that sometimes leukemia patients must be transfused with blood to replace the damaged cells.

We said good-bye, and left .

When we entered the car, I had my usual delayed reaction. A flood of tears welled up and overflowed and I cried brokenheartedly as I realized that the final chapter in Kathy's life was being written.

Janice and Christine were waiting at home with their sister, and I tried to control myself before I arrived there, for we agreed that we didn't want Kathy to sense that anything was wrong. This was nothing new, of course, for we tried to make a game of her ailments all the way through, so that she would not worry.

As we drove into the yard, the girls quickly opened the door. One look at our faces was all they needed. We all scattered and busied ourselves with other things. It was not the time for conversation. There was an observant little girl around, and we must not spoil these final days for her.

During the trying days when leukemia was working its havoc, I thought of the many happy experiences we had

had with Kathleen. I recalled the Children's Day program at church when she had recited, "Depart from evil and do good." We had waited with suspended breath. We needn't have worried, however, because she got through it fine. I remembered the parades that the girls had initiated, with banners and drums. Kathy was always the drum majorette. I thought of the dramatic plays they enjoyed producing, complete with costumes. I had to stop such reminiscing, or it would have driven me out of my mind.

We proved to be excellent actors. We grabbed Kathy at every opportunity and hugged her gaily. We planned all kinds of interesting activities. Then we looked at one another and wilted!

Janice's friend, Jerry Ruth, is a very fine photographer. He also has a tape recorder. The Saturday night following the diagnosis, we put both to good use. I wonder what Kathy thought of it all. She posed with each of us to "have her picture taken." We eagerly took as many as we dared, but she tired easily, so we had to be careful.

She loved the tape recorder. She was a real ham, and would sing in her little off-key way, and say proudly, "That's my boice." The letter *v* was a little difficult for her. The tape is one of our most precious treasures. We captured so much of her personality on it.

Charlie and Kathy had a difference of opinion about television programs. Her favorite was "The Three Stooges." They provoked her heartiest laughs. She hated any round table discussion on the air waves. She would protest vehemently to her father, "Turn the dial. Turn the dial."

On the tape that Saturday, Charlie purposely asked her what her favorite television program was. Then he suggested that it might be U. B. Round Table. "That's not fair," she shot back quickly. "That's for mens. Talk, talk, talk!" She repeated the Twenty-Third Psalm without much prompting, and she even consented to pray an earnest little prayer.

Janice and Chrissy sang, "You Are My Sunshine" with her, and it almost killed us all. Jerry made a quick exit to the kitchen to wipe his eyes.

When we played the tape back, Kathy sat on my lap to listen. When she heard herself, she looked at me with a sad little smile. Her voice hadn't sounded like she wanted it to. Later, that look was a comfort to me. I knew she was trying to say that she would like to do better. And she never could.

As soon as we knew that Kathy would not live, I dropped out of all outside activity. The neighborhood Bible class which I had taught continued to meet, but substitutes taught the lessons. The women of the class were very kind. They gave Nancy money to buy an Easter dress for Kathy. I think we all knew that it would be her burial dress. It was white, with blue trim.

If we had been careful of Kathy before this illness, we were doubly so now. Our nerves almost collapsed trying to keep her from "roughing it up." It wasn't long before large bruises began to appear on her body. Her gums and lips bled almost constantly. This troubled her a great deal. We moved her bed into our room so that we could watch her every minute. She had shared a room with Janice and Christine.

Every neighbor asked, "What can I do?" Then Mrs. Carter Lawson got an idea. She reasoned that if one card is good, a dozen are better, so she wrote a letter to the *Buffalo Evening News* requesting mail for "a sweet little neighbor girl who has acute leukemia." She included our address.

Little did she realize the avalanche of mail that this one request would bring. The mailman delivered Kathy's letters and packages in large grocery boxes. She received about 2500 in three weeks' time. An Italian newspaper down the state copied the address, and we received many letters and cards in that language. There were religious medals, at least 75 hankies, chewing gum, stuffed toys, and over fifty dollars from strangers. Several schools took Kathy as a project, with each pupil writing her a nice letter. It took us eight hours to open and read the notes and cards the first day. It was impossible to answer them all.

One woman, a stranger, was outstanding in her sympathy. Her name is Fran Murphy. After reading the article, she prepared an elaborate box with Kathy's name on the outside. In it she placed seven rather expensive gifts, marked for successive days of the week. The first thing Kathy did each morning was to run to the box and unwrap her gift for that day. We thought that was wonderful. But that wasn't all! The next Monday, Miss Murphy appeared with a second week's supply of gifts! She told us that her little brother had died of leukemia. He had slipped away while his mother was rocking him to sleep.

After Kathy's death, Charlie thought we should call Miss Murphy to tell her. She was waiting for her brother-in-law to bring her out with a third box for Kathy to enjoy. All this from a stranger. We learned much from Kathy's illness. Among other discoveries was this one: There are many, many fine people in the world.

Numerous friends had given Kathy presents through the years. Roy and Esther Tromburg gave her a beautiful dress. Carl and Ethel Olson often remembered her with gifts. These two couples and Eddie and Edna Lowe have been our "best friends" through the years.

When the Lowes heard the sad news, they brought Kathy the most gorgeous doll I have ever seen. It was a large bride doll with real nylon stockings, and even a veil. Kathy was starry-eyed over it. That evening Kathy went to church with us for the last time. Of course she had to take the doll along. We sat in our family pew, the last row in the church, as at other times. It was natural that all of the children in the service would look in Kathy's direction to admire the doll.

Kathy didn't like all of the staring. "Why don't they take their poogy eyes off of me?" she said. "Poogy" was a word she had originated when she wanted to say something naughty.

Those were especially hard days. I would look at Kathy and try to impress her every feature on my mind for the days ahead when she would be gone. She would eagerly hop on my lap whenever I sat down, for she was extremely affectionate, and as I hugged her I would think, "Some of these days I can't do this anymore." Oh, how we wished that we could keep her, but as with the Apostle Paul, so it was with Kathy — the time of her departure was "at hand." The Lord was gracious to shorten the time. We all knew that the knell would sound soon. Only the date remained unwritten.

Nothing that Dr. S. tried did any good. Each test showed a worse condition in the blood. We were thankful that she was not in any pain. The only complaint she made was that her ankle joint hurt a little bit. Her face became puffy as a result of the cortisone.

The John Lyon family stayed in close touch with us during this sad time. For four years I had taught an afternoon Bible class in Adele Lyon's living room, and we had become close friends. Kathy loved to go to their home with me. She teased Buddy. She played with the dolls and cribs which were brought downstairs especially for her. She latched onto Nancy Lyon every time we stopped by and begged, "Come home with me."

The eighteen members of the class did the over-and-above thing during Kathy's illness. They brought games for her and special foods to whet her appetite. Truly they proved to be "friends in need."

"Grandma" Root and Frances suffered with me, worrying about Kathy's condition. They kept in touch by telephone, asking in strained voices, "How is she today? Do you think she is any better?"

My poetry column in the local papers reflected my distress. Among the several poems which appeared was one entitled: "Sometime — But Not Yet." It described how we kept wishing that the time of Kathy's departure would be kept "sometime in the future." Mr. Jack Ogilvie, an announcer for a Buffalo television and radio station, saw it and called me, asking permission to use it on his Saturday-morning program. Many people of the area told me later that they had heard the poem.

We wished that we could grip the hands of the clock and hold back time. But it passed on relentlessly. The girls planned for the summer. They were sure that Kathy would be with us for picnics and swimming. I wasn't so sure. Somehow, I felt that everything was moving rapidly to a conclusion, especially in the light of the doctor's reports.

Charlie's family were wonderful — Bill and Lou in Florida, Fred and Win in Buffalo. These two brothers had been very kind to us since Kathy came, giving her presents and helping us in every way possible. Charlie's brother Don had died several years before, but Hazel and the family were also compassionate.

On Palm Sunday Charlie and the girls went to church. Kathy and I remained at home. She had worn pajamas most of the time around the house, but I decided to let her wear a pink-flowered nylon dress that Janice had bought for her. She looked so pretty with her yellow hair and fancy clothing.

Daddy and the girls were surprised when our little doll greeted them at the door. Feeling her importance, she came to the kitchen to help with the dinner. I can see her yet, carrying the dish of peas to the dining room for me. Then she seated everyone at the table. Dad was at the head of the table, and Kathy sat at his right. She was especially hungry and we were glad to see her eating roast beef in quantity.

During dinner, a telephone call came from Edna Lowe inviting us to go for a ride. Soon, Charlie, Kathy and I were riding along Broadway with our friends. The girls stayed at home, and when we returned they served us cake and coffee.

Kathy was tired and curled up on the davenport. Charlie sat beside her. After a while she motioned that she wanted to go upstairs to bed. This in itself was unusual. We usually had to coerce her to take naps. Dad, her obedient servant, didn't hesitate; he gathered her in his arms and tucked her in our big bed. She fell asleep right away.

After our company had gone, Charlie suggested that since Kathy was still sleeping, I should ride to church with Nancy. He persuaded me that it would be good for me to go and promised to keep Kathleen awake after her nap until I returned.

"It is hard to know what to do," I told Nancy as we rode along. "Maybe I shouldn't have left Kathy, but she couldn't be in better hands."

Our church organist, Joyce Hatch, was in Florida at the time, and Nancy was her assistant. As she began the prelude, Miss Violet McCollum touched me on the shoulder and said that Charlie wanted me to call him immediately.

I rushed to the church office telephone. He said, "When church is over, come right home. I don't want to alarm you, but when Kathy awakened, she couldn't bear weight on her leg. Stay for the service, but hurry home afterward."

My heart pounded, not only from the stairs I had climbed, but from the news. It didn't sound good.

While we were singing the first verse of the congregational hymn, I was again called to the telephone. This time Charlie was excited. "I called Dr. S., and he has ordered Kathy to Children's Hospital. She can't use either leg. Meet us there."

"How will you manage Kathy and drive, too?" I worried.

"I will lay her on the seat beside me," he said.

"No, don't try to do that." I was trying to keep my mind clear. "Ask Mrs. Kivett next door to ride with you and hold Kathy. We will meet you there right away."

As I went down the stairs again, I met our daughter-in-law, Carol. She was crying. "Isn't this awful?" she moaned.

"Yes, it is," and I patted her arm. "This may be it," I added.

Mr. Thornton White, a trustee in our church, met me in upper Fellowship Hall. "Is there any news?" he asked. I briefly told him, and he got word to the pastor. I learned later they paused for a time of prayer for Kathy and for us.

As soon as the song service was ended, Nancy, Christine and I sped to the hospital. In a comparatively short time, Jesse and Lucille Kivett drove up, bringing Charlie and Kathy. The Cheektowaga police had cleared the way for them. Kathy had been very ill all of the way, soiling her lovely gray wool coat and fluffy white hat. Charlie carried her into the emergency room and we removed the outer clothing. Kathy reached for my hand and put it to her lips to let me know that she knew I was there. As we watched, she lost consciousness rapidly, and soon she was no longer aware of her surroundings.

Resident doctors moved our little girl to more adequate surroundings, and I spoke to the doctors about the peace of heart that the Lord had given me in that sad hour.

Dr. S. came softly into the room and stood looking at Kathy. "This is it," he said, "unless a miracle occurs." He asked that they place her in a crib in a private room. Her breathing had become labored.

"It is at a time like this that a person is so glad for the hope of eternal life," I told the doctor. He nodded in agreement.

Pastor Swartz came to the hospital after the church

service had ended. He told us that Bud and Mary White were in the chapel downstairs praying. We were so grateful. As time passed, Janice and Jerry came and took their place with Nancy and Christine in the waiting room. Then Carol and David joined them.

The pastor offered a prayer of committal of Kathleen's soul to God. I sat near her, holding her hand in mine, with my other hand placed over her enlarged heart. Charlie sat just at her head. We exchanged Scripture verses of comfort as we watched. "For we know that if the earthly house of our tabernacle be dissolved, we have a building from God, a house not made with hands, eternal, in the heavens," I quoted. "To be absent from the body . . . [is] to be present with the Lord."

"To depart and be with Christ is far better," the pastor said.

Charlie's favorite was, "Peace I leave with you, my peace I give unto you: not as the world giveth, give I unto you. Let not your heart be troubled, neither let it be afraid."

After a while Charlie decided to tell the girls not to wait. He thought we might be there all night, so he went downstairs to give them the message. While he was gone, Kathy stopped breathing. "Is she gone?" the pastor whispered.

"No, her heart is still beating," I told him. That sturdy heart, which had caused us so much worry in Kathy's lifetime, continued to beat at least a full minute after her final breath.

Just then Charlie reentered the room. I told him Kathy was gone. He was shocked at the finality. "I wouldn't have gone," he began, but we both knew that God had taken Kathy when it was His time.

A nurse covered Kathy's face. Before we left the room, Charlie uncovered her face and kissed her cheek. We walked out into the hall together.

A resident doctor made the necessary arrangements for

us. When they were completed, he said a rather startling thing, "If you think your grief is great, you should see the parents of defective children who have not been good to them. At least, you did everything in your power to give your child a good life. Some parents resent the child and mistreat it. Then when the child finally dies, their consciences become acutely alive, and their remorse is terrible." I had never thought of that.

Pastor Swartz took us home. It was the first time since Kathy's birth that Charlie and I had left her at a hospital and walked out together. My feet were leaden. How could I leave her there? Then I thought, "I am really not leaving her here. She is safe with the Lord."

And I was comforted.

CHAPTER 18

The Long Walk of Faith Ended

IT WAS ALL OVER — the long walk of faith.

Kathy was like a fragile doll in her white casket. We brought her home, and she lay in our living room, surrounded by several beautiful baskets of flowers. The neighborhood class sent a tiny bouquet of rosebuds which we placed in her hand. A small cross, made of rosebuds, came from Mr. and Mrs. Richard Bennett and the employees of the *Herald* and *Enterprise*. Charlie and I ordered a floral arrangement of pink and white roses, heart-shaped. A blanket of roses was the love gift of her brother and sisters. Others sent contributions of money to the Heart Association, the Cancer Society, and to Prospect Avenue Baptist Church.

Hundreds of people came to offer condolences. Over fifty policemen came, friends of Charlie. Buffalo Police Chief Frank Felicetta was among them. As he stood near the casket, he remarked, "You expect old people to die. They have lived their lives. But a child? My God!"

A station wagon brought "the girls" from Charlie's precinct. They were the crossing guards. Helen Adamski came in first. She was the "mother" of the group. They all told me what a fine man their boss was. I agreed. I am married to him!

Kathy's Aunt Lucille, for whom she received her second

name, came from Indiana for the funeral. "You have no regrets," she said. "You took wonderful care of her."

As people crowded in, there was confusion, and my mind would hardly comprehend the situation. I caught myself looking around to see if Kathy was all right. It would be a long time before I would quit listening for her. Every person had some kind word, some sympathetic remark to make. One, however, outshone all others for me. It was made by Molly Stock, the wife of Hugh Stock, a teacher of music at Depew High School. She came quietly to my side, and gazed at the form of our little one. All she said was, "There was never a child loved more."

The Sticht family came to pay their respects. Afterward, Charlie walked out to the road with them. "We believe Kathy is in Heaven," he remarked.

"Well, if she didn't make it, there is no hope for the rest of us," Ed observed. When they reached home, Michael, who was thirteen, said, "Some of these days I am going to cry real hard about Kathy. My throat hurts from holding back the tears."

After everyone had gone, the night before the funeral, I found Janice sobbing in her room. "She was my pal," she cried.

I reminded her that this was in God's hands. "But we have waited and waited for spring," she told me, "and now spring is here, and Kathy is gone."

"Heaven is better than spring," I said. It was a sudden thought, but it helped us both to remember it.

Pastor Swartz gave a simple funeral sermon, very comforting. We laid Kathy's body in Lancaster Rural Cemetery. The pastor's prayer at the grave was unique. "Mark this place," he prayed. "This is one of your saints. And when you return for your own, remember this dear one." Later, we placed a small tombstone at the grave, flanked by two

Japanese yew trees. Carved on the marble slab are these words: "She loved the Lord."

Kathy's story may not be really completed for many years. The influence of her life goes on and on. During her illness, Janice received a letter from Donna Singer. She wrote in part, "I am shocked to learn of Kathy's illness. I want you to know how sincerely I have admired all of you for the way you have so wholeheartedly made Kathy a part of the family. I thought you would like to know that I have changed my course at Syracuse University and plan to teach exceptional children, because of Kathy."

The year of Kathy's death, Janice attended graduation exercises at Court Street School. "It is a shame that there is no award to be given to the retarded children," she thought. They could not even qualify for perfect attendance, because they are afflicted with illnesses of one kind or another. She mentioned the thought to Mr. Perrine.

"I was thinking the same thing," the principal said. "We could set up an award of some kind and call it the Kathy Schultz award."

Janice told her father about it. His eyes shone. "We will finance it," he promised. And so, for the next ten years, at least, a child from the special class will receive the Kathy Schultz Award for Good Citizenship. It will be a silver dollar.

We have heard of the salvation of several children in Sunday school who were told Kathy's story by their teachers.

On Easter Sunday the next year, we placed flowers in the pulpit in memory of loved ones and Janice bought a special plant for Kathy. As we casually read the list of those who placed flowers, we were very pleased to see that Hannah Galloway also sent a plant in memory of Kathy. "She is the nearest thing to a little sister that I shall ever have," Hannah explained to us later. "She was a tease to us, but I loved her."

One of the secretaries at C—— Hospital told us later that Kathy's case will make medical history because she progressed so far mentally. "You should see some of the cases that come in here," she told me. "Then you would appreciate all the more how wonderful your Kathy was."

I was asked by a Depew woman to write to her mother because of the death of a seven-year-old son, killed by an automobile. One of the things I wrote was: "Who is there to say that your son and my daughter did not live their lives as fully as people who live to be seventy?" In some ways I believe that Kathy accomplished more, limited though she was.

I have learned many things by this experience. One of the most important lessons is to be careful to stay in the will of God at all times. Then we are on "praying ground" in times of trouble. Trouble comes to the whole human family. When it comes, it is of utmost importance to find the mind of God in the matter. I found that through the study of God's Word one can walk by faith and know without doubting that the Lord will bring to pass that which He has promised. In the spirit of the Hebrew children of old (Daniel 6:17-18), we must say, "If He will deliver me . . . well. But, if not, I will still trust Him."

How we have missed our little joy! She was truly our sunshine. None of us can get used to being without her. When Janice goes into a department store, she naturally gravitates to the dresses in Kathy's size. Then she remembers. Chris carefully protects Kathy's toys and books from the careless hands of the grandchildren. Dad sits on the bench back of the house and imagines his Katie is swinging nearby or playing in the sandbox.

As for me — We persuaded Dad to take a trip to Detroit about three months after Kathy's death. The Hains family had moved there and we thought a short vacation would be good for us all.

We arrived in Detroit at supper time and stopped at a restaurant to eat before driving out to the home of our friends. We had to wait for a table. At last the hostess came to us. "How many are there of you?" she asked. "Five," I replied automatically. She looked at me rather startled, and I looked around, confused. There are only four of us now.

A friend of ours visited us one evening recently. A remark she made confirmed Kathy's story in a beautiful way. She said, "I had never heard that a defective child could be a joy until I read Dale Evans' book and later saw Kathy. You didn't have to tell people what she meant to you. Everyone could see it. We all loved her, too, and she was definitely a joy."

That was what the Lord had promised when He gave Kathleen to us. And He always keeps his word.

My china cup no longer is a token of an unfulfilled promise. It is now a reminder of the years of happiness we had when God sent a joy into our home, a little girl named Kathy.

P*oems*

Kathy Goes to the Hospital

Kathy has a special story
  She is telling one and all
Of a journey she is taking
  To a hospital this fall.
She and Mommy talk about it;
  They have planned it, every part,
From the afternoon she enters
  'Til the doctor "fix my heart."

Kathy makes her sisters listen
  As again, she must rehearse
All about the tests and Xrays
  With attention from the nurse.
"She will wheel me to the doctor
  On a lovely little cart,
'Cause he's going to make me better
  When he fixes up my heart!"
"Please prepare her," they advise us,
  "Make her understanding clear.
If she knows the full procedure,
  It will quiet any fear."
Who prepares the worried parents
  When the operations start?
God alone can calm the spirit
  While they're "fixing up" her heart.

Invalid

God sent a joy into our home,
  With silken golden hair.
He plainly labeled "fragile,
  Handle her with loving care."
We welcomed her and read the tags,
  We pledged to try our best
To follow all instructions,
  Trusting God to do the rest.

God sent a joy into our home,
  A walking, talking joy,
A beam of brightest sunshine
  When dark shadows would annoy,
But we have learned, in nurturing
  This child so frail and sweet,
The place (a strange and sacred spot)
  Where joy and sorrow meet.

Many More Happy Birthdays

Seven little people sing a "Happy Birthday" song.
Seven little candles on the fancy cake belong.
Seven little packages are opened, one by one.
Seven little pairs of eyes are sparkling with fun.
Seven little scoops of ice cream rest upon the plates.
Seven little hungry mouths (and not a one who waits!)
Seven little children wishing Kathy "many more."
"Precious Jesus, let it be," we silently implore.

The Two of Them

With small blond head content on Daddy's arm,
  The two of them reread the Golden Book.
The knowing "word for word" gives added charm.
  They scarce at any sentence need to look.
It is not what they read that matters much
  It is the hug and punctuated kiss,
The pat of cheek by Kathy's gentle touch
  That causes Dad to treasure hours of this.
It is a sacred time for both of them
  As they enjoy the stories old and new.
Of Daddy's jewels, she, his dearest gem,
  Brings Heaven near to earth when day is through.
The simple nursery rhymes create the power
  Of magic when repeated by the pair.
The books and love assure a happy hour
  For Dad and Kathy in their special chair.

Sometime — But Not Yet

We borrowed a child from the treasury of Heaven.
  We know she is loaned, though we sometimes forget
Until there's a hint of reclaiming this treasure,
  Then hearts cry out quickly, "Dear Father, not yet!"

The child has brought joy to our home by her coming
  We're glad to have kept her. There is no regret.
We selfishly guard her, and though we can't keep her
  Forever, we whisper, "Please, Father, not yet!"

We know that the day we have dreaded approaches.
  We try to accept it without whine or fret,
And pray that the Lord will forgive us for praying
  Again and again and again, "Oh, not yet!"

Heaven is Better Than Spring

We watched for the springtime together
   Throughout the long winter, so cold.
We wished for the grass and the flowers
   With dandelions spattering gold.
We hoped for the budding of lilacs,
   We listened for robins to sing.
We watched and we wished and we waited —
   But Heaven is better than spring.

We planned for a bed of petunias.
   We thought of the crocus in bloom.
We mentioned the roses we'd gather
   To add a fresh touch to our room.
We dreamed of vacation-time picnics:
   The sandbox, the slides, and the swing,
And found them to be an illusion,
   For Heaven is better than spring.

We selfishly mourn that she left us.
   We think of the things we could share,
But God gives a sweet consolation
   And lifts us above the despair.
There's no pain or sorrow or darkness
   Within the bright realm of our King.
There's joy and sweet peace there forever,
   And Heaven is better than spring.

The Golden Stair

When angels sweep the golden stair,
　　Do they find any clutter there?
A twig from off the tree of life;
　　A gifted angel's shining fife;
A gem left over from a crown,
　　Or children skipping up and down?
Are angels patient with the shriek
　　Of children playing hide-and-seek?

When angels sweep the golden stair,
　　Do they find Kathy's dollies there
Propped safely on the velvet tread
　　While she slides bannisters instead?
No longer weary, weak and sore,
　　Released to play forevermore.
No wracking cough to spoil her play,
　　Just joy and love and endless day.

When angels sweep the golden stair,
　　Do they hear childish questions there?
"When will my Mama come?" she asks
　　Of angels busy with their tasks.
"Does Daddy still remember me
　　When he observes our cedar tree?"
God bless our baby waiting there
　　To greet us on the golden stair.

No Replacement

I tucked a brown-eyed girl into bed,
  Where a blond child used to sleep.
We shared a story of Goldilocks
  From the Golden Books we keep.
She said her prayers in her childish way,
  And I kissed the rounded cheek,
While memory crowded me all about
  So strongly I could not speak.

I love this tiny and fragile girl
  (Her own mother's miniature),
And carefully granted every wish
  To cause her to feel secure.
I showed her how to adjust the light,
  Which hung near the big bed's side.
(She could not have understood my grief
  Or the unshed tears I cried.)

I pressed a bunny in her small arms
  (The toy of the other child).
I prayed that she couldn't see beneath
  The mask, as I looked and smiled.
There was no need to destroy the fun
  A night at Grandma's can be —
But no one can fill the special place
  Of the blond one, lost to me.

The Message of Silence

A noisy silence shouts throughout the quiet, empty place.
  We hold our ears to hush it and its message to erase.
Each corner of the room reechoes still the loud refrain,
  While objects, once inanimate, repeat the sounds again.

Mute silence owns a rasping voice and forces us to hear.
  Its solemn quiet blasts the news that grates the mourner's **ear.**
The sober silence clamors on the empty house to fill —
  So ruthless and unbearable and still . . . . . . so very still.

Little Girls Go To School

Mothers are shopping for dresses and ribbons,
  For crinolines, sweaters and slippers and socks.
Mothers are storing supplies of new groceries
  To have food for sandwiches packed in each box.
Mothers are washing and ironing and sewing.
  The lovely starched dresses are hung in a row.
Summer vacation has passed very quickly,
  Reluctantly children to classes must go.

Oh, what a hurry and bustle each morning
  When hair must be braided or rolled into curls.
There is so much to attend to by mothers.
  In dressing and pressing for their little girls.
Lastly, the brushing of teeth is important,
  Performed while she stands on a small wooden stool.
How do I know about every procedure?
  I once sent a golden-haired daughter to school.

Remembering Kathy

Will there come a day when I look away
  With a dull, unseeing eye
When a blue-eyed youngster with golden hair
  Runs gaily, hurriedly by?
Will the morning dawn when I cease to strain
  My ears for her voice so sweet?
Will I ever learn not to quickly turn
  At the skip of childish feet?

Will it ever be that the small girl's rack
  In the stores where I must go
Will cease to tear at the grief I bear
  As they do now, row by row?
Will the quiet house ever seem to be
  The norm? (Not so out of tune.)
Will I cease to moan when I lunch alone
  In the silent place at noon?

Will my mind adjust to the cruel truth
  That no child demands my care?
Will I ever be from the thought set free
  That "she, too, must have her share"?
She has left so much of herself with me,
  Though she could no longer stay,
That in fancy wild, every bright-eyed child
  Is Kathy, again, at play.

A Year — Eternity

We reached the fork of the pleasant road
  With our little Kathy Lu,
Then she branched off on the path marked "Home"
  While we must continue through.
She waved "good-bye" with her frail white hand
  As she hurried on the way,
Nor could the devoted love we gave
  Coax our little one to stay.

Our walk had been a delightful one,
  For she charmed us with her smile.
We tried to give her a lifetime's joy,
  Crowded into that short while,
But when we reached the fork of the road,
  We watched her pass on from sight,
And felt the magnet of Heaven's door
  Compelling her toward its light.

A year has passed, such a lonesome year,
  For she was our darling pet.
Sometimes we fancy we hear her step
  On the stairway, even yet.
But then, we notice her empty desk,
  Uncluttered with books and muss.
A year is a moment there, I know,
  And so endless, here, to us.